IMMERSION
Bible Studies

1 & 2 SAMUEL
1 & 2 KINGS
1 & 2 CHRONICLES

Praise for IMMERSION

"IMMERSION BIBLE STUDIES is a powerful tool in helping readers to hear God speak through Scripture and to experience a deeper faith as a result."
Adam Hamilton, author of *24 Hours That Changed the World*

"If you're looking for a deeper knowledge and understanding of God's Word, you must dive into IMMERSION BIBLE STUDIES. Whether in a group setting or as an individual, you will experience God and his unconditional love for each of us in a whole new way."
Pete Wilson, founding and senior pastor of Cross Point Church

"This beautiful series helps readers become fluent in the words and thoughts of God, for purposes of illumination, strength building, and developing a closer walk with the One who loves us so."
Laurie Beth Jones, author of *Jesus, CEO* and *The Path*

"The IMMERSION BIBLE STUDIES series is no less than a game changer. It ignites the purpose and power of Scripture by showing us how to do more than just know God or love God; it gives us the tools to love like God as well."
Shane Stanford, author of *You Can't Do Everything . . . So Do Something*

"I highly commend to you IMMERSION BIBLE STUDIES, which tells us what the Bible teaches and how to apply it personally."
John Ed Mathison, author of *Treasures of the Transformed Life*

IMMERSION
Bible Studies

1 & 2 SAMUEL
1 & 2 KINGS
1 & 2 CHRONICLES

Timothy B. Cargal

Abingdon Press

Nashville

1 & 2 SAMUEL, 1 & 2 KINGS, 1 & 2 CHRONICLES
IMMERSION BIBLE STUDIES
by Timothy B. Cargal

Library of Congress Cataloging-in-Publication Data

Cargal, Timothy B. (Timothy Boyd)
 1 & 2 Samuel, 1 & 2 Kings, 1 & 2 Chronicles / Timothy B. Cargal.
  pages cm — (Immersion Bible studies)
 Includes bibliographical references and index.
 ISBN 978-1-4267-1635-5 (curriculum—printed / text plus-cover : alk.
paper) 1. Bible. O.T. Samuel—Textbooks. 2. Bible. O.T.
Kings—Textbooks. 3. Bible. O.T. Chronicles—Textbooks. I. Title. II.
Title: First and Second Samuel, First and Second Kings, First and
Second Chronicles. III. Title: First and Second Samuel, First and Second Kings,.
 BS1325.5.C37 2012
 222'.06—dc23

2012017453

Editor: Stan Purdum
Leader Guide Writer: Martha Bettis Gee

12 13 14 15 16 17 18 19 20 21—10 9 8 7 6 5 4 3 2 1

Manufactured in the United States of America

Contents

Review Team

Diane Blum
Pastor
East End United Methodist Church
Nashville, Tennessee

Susan Cox
Pastor
McMurry United Methodist Church
Claycomo, Missouri

Margaret Ann Crain
Professor of Christian Education
Garrett-Evangelical Theological Seminary
Evanston, Illinois

Nan Duerling
Curriculum Writer and Editor
Cambridge, Maryland

Paul Escamilla
Pastor and Writer
St. John's United Methodist Church
Austin, Texas

James Hawkins
Pastor and Writer
Smyrna, Delaware

Andrew Johnson
Professor of New Testament
Nazarene Theological Seminary
Kansas City, Missouri

Snehlata Patel
Pastor
Woodrow United Methodist Church
Staten Island, New York

Emerson B. Powery
Professor of New Testament
Messiah College
Grantham, Pennsylvania

Clayton Smith
Pastoral Staff
Church of the Resurrection
Leawood, Kansas

Harold Washington
Professor of Hebrew Bible
Saint Paul School of Theology
Kansas City, Missouri

Carol Wehrheim
Curriculum Writer and Editor
Princeton, New Jersey

IMMERSION BIBLE STUDIES

A fresh new look at the Bible, from beginning to end,
and what it means in your life.

Welcome to IMMERSION!

We've asked some of the leading Bible scholars, teachers, and pastors to help us with a new kind of Bible study. IMMERSION remains true to Scripture but always asks, "Where are you in your life? What do you struggle with? What makes you rejoice?" Then it helps you read the Scriptures to discover their deep, abiding truths. IMMERSION is about God and God's Word, and it is also about you—not just your thoughts, but your feelings and your faith.

In each study you will prayerfully read the Scripture and reflect on it. Then you will engage it in three ways:

Claim Your Story
Through stories and questions, think about your life, with its struggles and joys.

Enter the Bible Story
Explore Scripture and consider what God is saying to you.

Live the Story
Reflect on what you have discovered, and put it into practice in your life.

IMMERSION makes use of an exciting new translation of Scripture, the Common English Bible (CEB). The CEB and IMMERSION BIBLE STUDIES will offer adults:

- the emotional expectation to find the love of God
- the rational expectation to find the knowledge of God
- reliable, genuine, and credible power to transform lives
- clarity of language

Whether you are using the Common English Bible or another translation, IMMERSION BIBLE STUDIES will offer a refreshing plunge into God's Word, your life, and your life with God.

1.

Samuel's Journey With God

1 Samuel 1–15

Claim Your Story

The ways in which we as a culture think and talk about our lives together before God are changing. One primary example of this change, according to pollsters, is the number of people in America who now describe themselves as being "spiritual, not religious." Although it does not show up in the polling data as much, another example would be how frequently people describe their faith lives as a "journey." Often these two trends converge. People tell the stories about their spiritual experiences with God over the years—about moments or periods in life when God seemed near and alive to them, and about other times when God seemed distant at best or completely absent at worst.

Such personal stories share much in common with the biblical stories. Some might speak longingly about what it would have been like to live in "Bible times" when people heard God's voice as audibly as that of a person in the next room. But the reality is that even heroes of faith such as Samuel did not always recognize God's Spirit calling to them (1 Samuel 3:1-10). They too struggled in their journey through life, trying to remain engaged with God and to discern God's purposes. Listening closely to their stories can help us better understand how to stay engaged with God in our own spiritual journeys.

In what ways is your spiritual life a journey? How do you ascertain God's purposes for your life?

Enter the Bible Story

Samuel is the title character, if you will, of two books within our Bibles. Some measure of his importance and influence may be gained from the fact that the stories within those two books extend decades beyond his death. As we shall see, Samuel was a transitional leader in Israel's history—one of the last of its judges and the anointer of its first two kings. But Samuel also served in roles most often associated with priests and prophets within that culture and was even dedicated as a child to a lifelong vow of special commitment to God as a nazirite. According the *Bible Dictionary* of the Common English Bible, "Nazirites demonstrated their devotion to God through distinctive behaviors, commonly observing prohibitions against cutting the hair, drinking wine, or touching the dead."

You might think that with all these things going for him, Samuel must have lived an especially blessed life. Wouldn't it be great if our own spiritual journeys included moments when we heard God's voice, received the accolades of God's people, and were confident of not only God's will for the world but also that we were playing a part in bringing it to fruition? But as we travel Samuel's journey along with him, we see that the details of his walk with God included valleys as well as mountaintop experiences.

About the Scriptures

In the Common English Bible (like all Christian Bibles), the stories about the rise and fall of Israel's and Judah's kings are told in six books: First and Second Samuel, First and Second Kings, and First and Second Chronicles. We will look at the relationship between First and Second Chronicles and these other books in the last chapter of this study. For now, we need to understand two things about the four books of Samuel and Kings.

First, in the Hebrew Bible, there are only two books with the titles "Samuel" and "Kings" respectively. Samuel's story is basically contained in the first sixteen of the fifty-five total chapters of the book(s) bearing his name (his death is recounted in 1 Samuel 25:1, but his last mention comes in a story about Saul summoning his spirit from the grave in 1 Samuel 28). Many surmise the whole book is named for Samuel because it deals with the two kings he anointed, Saul and David.

Second, the books of Samuel and Kings are widely considered parts of a larger work referred to by scholars as the Deuteronomistic History. It includes the books of Joshua and Judges as well. It can be helpful to think of Samuel as one of Israel's last judges (see 1 Samuel 7:15-17). One of the patterns in this "history" is how it relates cycles of when God's people rejected the Lord, suffered as a result, repented, and were restored by God only to have the cycle repeat. Watch for signs of this pattern as we read through First and Second Samuel and First and Second Kings.

Samuel's Birth and Dedication (1 Samuel 1:1–2:11)

One of the realities of spiritual journeys is that things that seem so clear and obvious in a scriptural story or even in the way a family member or friend recounts an experience after the fact were actually much more uncertain in the moment. If you pay close attention to all the details of the story, glimpses of that original ambiguity can come through—and sometimes the very point of the story seems to be to remind us that not everything is clear. Such is the case with the story of Samuel's birth. Let's begin, then, by shifting our own gaze a bit. Let's recognize that the opening of First Samuel isn't really Samuel's story; it is Hannah's story. And Hannah is nothing if not misunderstood.

Hannah's story, as we read it in Scripture, follows a definite and well-established pattern. She is the beloved wife who longs for but has not been able to give birth to a child. That story line places her in some fairly heady company: she is preceded by Sarah and Rachel in Genesis and followed by Elizabeth in Luke. Because we know their stories, we are confident we know hers as well. But Hannah didn't know her story would eventually be told alongside theirs. She only knew she wanted a son. Her husband, Elkanah, tried to console her: "Aren't I worth more to you than ten sons?" (1:8). His words were almost certainly intended to be comforting, but probably would have been heard as patronizing or even somewhat belittling. Perhaps she heard in his voice echoes of Elkanah's other wife, Peninnah—who had both sons and daughters and had become "her rival"—who "would make fun of her mercilessly, just to bother her" (1:6).

Even the priest Eli ridiculed Hannah (1:9-18). She was at the Lord's house and so overwhelmed with emotion that she was "praying in her heart; her lips were moving, but her voice was silent, so Eli thought she was drunk." His command to her was simple and direct: "Sober up!" But by that point, she had had enough. "No sir!" she replied, "Don't think your servant is some good-for-nothing woman. This whole time I've been praying out of my great worry and trouble!" It's hard to know just what tone Eli took when he told her, "Then go in peace. And may the God of Israel give you what you've asked from him." Was he embarrassed for his misunderstanding or dismissive of what he took as an unlikely cover story? Even Hannah's final words in the exchange—"Please think well of me, your servant"—can be taken in two very different ways. Was she chastened by the priest's harshness and pleading for forgiveness and understanding or hoping her newly acquired ally would continue to remember her in her agony for a child? When you notice in the Common English Bible's footnote in verse 18 that the Hebrew text lacks the description that as Hannah left she "wasn't sad any longer," then you are only left to wonder.

Across the Testaments

Hannah's Prayer

Hannah's prayer is the model for Mary's prayer in Luke 1:46-55, traditionally called the Magnificat. Though the circumstances of their pregnancies were opposite (Hannah, the wife who waited years for a son; Mary, pregnant even before her wedding), both women's stories are built on the foundation that those around them were certain God had abandoned them. Both women's prayers extol the truth that God is with those whom many think are forsaken.

Then, with only the certainty a narrator can provide, we are told, "the LORD remembered her" (1:19). Did Eli remember or "think well" of her? (Not if Hannah's reintroduction of herself to him in 1:26-28 offers any clue.) Did Elkanah think there would be any different consequence of their sexual relations than before? (Not if his still condescending tone in 1:23 is any indication.) But all that really mattered was "the LORD remembered her." And once she cradled a son in her arms as the matriarchs Sarah and Rachel had, Hannah remembered and knew of a certainty that God was the source of her joy. So, "she named him Samuel, which means 'I asked the LORD for him'" (1:20).

Hannah also remembered her promise that if God would give her a son, she would "give him to the LORD for his entire life" as a nazirite (1:11, 22-23). Once she had weaned the child (likely at an age somewhat older than we wean our children), she kept that promise. When she left him at "the LORD's house at Shiloh," she offered a prayer full of confidence that God is the one ultimately in control (2:1-10). Every conventional sign of power is only an illusion before the Lord. Those who place confidence in themselves fail to see it, but everything is dependent upon God's purpose. It is a prayer far removed in every way from her earlier prayer "out of...great worry and trouble" (1:16).

Samuel's Rise to Prominence (1 Samuel 2:12–7:17)

Samuel's own journey is paved not only by his mother's faithfulness but also by the faithlessness of others. As the very young Samuel is being raised at "the LORD's house" under the supervision of Eli, the priest's own sons were earning a reputation for corruption (2:15-17). In contrast, "the boy Samuel grew up in the LORD's service" (2:21b). As the years passed, Eli's sons moved on to radically inappropriate sexual behavior (2:22); "meanwhile, the boy Samuel kept growing up and was more and more liked by both the LORD and the people" (2:26). These contrasts, along with an oracle from "a man of God" that God had rejected Eli's sons as legitimate priests for Israel (2:27-36), provide the backdrop for Samuel's call story.

The story is actually quite comic in its telling (3:1-19). Three times during the night, God calls out Samuel's name, and three times Samuel runs off to Eli thinking that it was the priest who was summoning him. Twice the narrator tries to explain Samuel's failure to recognize that it is God who was calling him (3:1b, 7), but the explanations do little to reduce the humor of the story. It is only on a third occasion of being awakened that a possibility dawned on Eli that still eluded Samuel: "If he calls you, say 'Speak, LORD. Your servant is listening'" (3:9).

We can draw two lessons as we chuckle at Samuel (and ourselves, if we admit it). First, if even heroes of the faith had difficulty distinguishing the voice of the Spirit from other voices in their lives, then we shouldn't be too hard on ourselves if we only recognize God's directing voice in looking back over the course of our journey. Second—and just as importantly—we should acknowledge that we need the assistance of others experienced in the faith to help us discern when the voice we are hearing really is God calling to us.

The message God brought to Samuel that night reasserted the earlier message brought by the "man of God" about the rejection of Eli's sons. It not only confirmed that that man was a prophet but also began to establish Samuel's own prophetic credentials, especially since over the coming years "the LORD was with him, not allowing any of his words to fail" (3:19).

At this point, the story line in Samuel takes a three-chapter-long sidetrack away from Samuel's own journey. But this story about how the Philistines came to first capture and then subsequently return "the chest containing the LORD's covenant" is no simple meanwhile-back-at-the-ranch literary diversion. It recounts both how the demise of Eli's sons, Hophni and Phineas, came about and through its echoes connects with stories from Judges when Israel had previously failed in its covenant responsibilities to God, repented of those failures, and God had yet again come to their aid. And as before, even that deliverance was not enough to secure Israel's allegiance to the covenant; for when the story returns to Samuel, some "twenty years" later, we find him calling on the people to "get rid of all the foreign gods" to whom they had given their hearts so

About the Christian Faith

The Ebenezer

The renewal of the covenant at Mizpah within this story provides the background to a strange sounding line in the hymn, "Come, Thou Fount of Every Blessing." In the second stanza, we sing, "Here I raise mine Ebenezer; hither by thy help I'm come." The Ebenezer ("stone of help") was a monument erected to commemorate—"The Lord helped us to this very point" (7:12)—and to bear witness to future generations about the covenant renewed there (compare Joshua 24:25-27). The hymn reminds us to see that God is the one who has been with us in the past and who will be the source of all goodness and blessing in our future lives.

that in response to their repentance, God would once more save them from the Philistines (7:2-14).

So it was that the prophet Samuel also "served as Israel's judge his whole life" (7:15-17). But it was at the end of his life's journey that it would take its most unexpected turn—not just once, but twice.

Samuel and the Beginning of Israel's Monarchy (1 Samuel 8-15)

As Samuel grew old, his hope was that his sons would continue down the road he had been traveling. So "he appointed his sons to serve as Israel's judges" (8:1). But Joel and Abijah proved to be just as corrupt as Eli's sons had been a generation earlier, and the elders of Israel refused to accept their leadership. Instead, they requested that he appoint a king to rule over them "like all the other nations have" (8:5). Samuel thought it was a bad idea. As God pointed out in response to Samuel's prayer for guidance, this was only the latest in a long string of the people's rejection of God's reign over them stretching back to just days after they had left Egypt. Although God told Samuel to try to persuade them it was a bad idea by reminding them what life under a king was really like, God also conceded there was no real chance such persuasion would succeed. When in fact it did fail, God told Samuel, "Comply with their request. Give them a king" (8:22).

God's directive was simple and straightforward. The process itself proved to be anything but. The humor in the story returns, although it is somewhat subtler. Yet how else than as humor is one to understand a story about the son of a wealthy man, handsome and standing "head and shoulders above everyone else" (9:2), who fails at rounding up his father's stray donkeys but nevertheless winds up anointed as king of Israel? Might there be just a touch of political satire against kings mixed in this humor? Even once anointed as king, Saul declined to share anything with his family other than Samuel's assurances that the donkeys—that are not with him— had nevertheless been found. When Samuel summons Israel to present Saul as their king, Saul is ultimately found "hiding among the supplies." Or was he trying to hide, since again we are told, "he was head and shoulders taller than anyone else" (10:22b-23)? Little wonder, then, that some of the people "despised Saul" (10:27). Only once, when Saul succeeded in a military campaign to break a siege on Jabesh-gilead, did Israel truly follow Samuel in accepting Saul as their king (11:1-15).

Thinking that at last his work with Israel was over, Samuel once again reminded the people both of their past failures and of God's gracious response to their repentance (12:6-15). The prospects for the future under the king could be bright, but only if they would "fear the LORD and serve him faithfully with all [their] heart." If they instead repeated their past errors, Samuel told the people, "then both you and your king will be destroyed" (12:24-25). The ensuing chapters (13–15) recount the events whereby first the promise of a dynasty and ultimately the authority from God to reign itself would be stripped away from Saul. But through it all, Samuel stayed engaged with God, praying for the people and listening for God's voice to direct him on his continuing journey (see, for example, 15:10-11).

Live the Story

We began by considering the similarities between the biblical stories and our stories, by reminding ourselves that these stories can help us better understand our life journeys. As we think about how we can live out these insights, we need to also remind ourselves how the very telling of the story brings clarity that was almost certainly lacking in the moment.

The old saying goes, "Hindsight is 20-20." So it is with our spiritual lives. The scriptural stories provide us with corrective lenses. The stories about Hannah, Samuel, and all the rest bring into sharper focus the ways God is at work in our personal lives and the world more broadly. But it is just as true that it is in looking back over our own journeys through those lenses that we are able to see God's presence most clearly.

Take some time to reflect back over your life not just as a sequence of events but also as a spiritual journey. How does Samuel's story help you give structure and insight into your telling of your own story, whether to yourself or to others? How do Hannah's prayers help you share your own struggles with God?

2.

Living Faithfully

1 Samuel 16–31

Claim Your Story

My wife and I are blessed with two children, a son and a daughter born eight years apart. Being of different genders and broadly separated in ages, one might think we were spared many of the fights so common between siblings. Perhaps we were spared "many," but certainly not all of them. I had plenty of opportunities to separate my oldest from his sister, assure him I would be talking to her next, but then once again explain that it really didn't matter what his toddler (and later elementary school-aged) sister had done to him. He was so much older, so I had to have different expectations of him. "You are only responsible for what you did," I would say, "no matter whether what she did was wrong or not."

We all need to be reminded occasionally about both the limits of what we can and cannot control and the importance of taking responsibility for what we can. Just as importantly, we need to join our faith in God to our personal accountability. When we are in a faithful relationship with God, it's easier to be faithful in our relationships with others, because we trust God to do what we can't.

When have you wished you could change or control how others behaved? When have you had to face your own responsibility for problems in a relationship? How has your faith in God affected how you responded in such situations?

Enter the Bible Story

David was by far the youngest of Jesse's eight sons. We can only imagine how many disputes Jesse broke up. But I wonder: Did David overhear conversations between Jesse and his brothers like the ones I've had with my son? One thing is certain from considering David's interactions with Saul: Somewhere along the line, he learned that while he wasn't responsible for what others did to him, he had to take responsibility for what he did in return. And a key reason that he may have been able to do that was because "David, Jesse's son, [was] *a man who shares [God's] desires*" (literally, "after my heart"; Acts 13:22).

Samuel Anoints David to Be King (1 Samuel 16:1-13)

Although Samuel had thought having a king was a bad idea for Israel (1 Samuel 8:6), he nevertheless took no pleasure when the course of events proved his concerns fully justified. He grieved at Saul's failure, and God had to prod him to move on (16:1). So it was that he traveled to Bethlehem so that he could anoint one of Jesse's sons to be the next king of Israel.

Yet despite all that had transpired with Saul, Samuel seems to have fallen back into the same trap of expectations with regard to what makes a person fit to be a king. As soon as Samuel saw Eliab among Jesse's sons, he concluded, "that must be the LORD's anointed right in front" (16:6). But God didn't have either Eliab or any of his six strapping brothers in mind. Everyone may have previously fixated on Saul's regal bearing as he stood "head and shoulders above everyone else" (9:2; see also 10:23), but this time God stressed, "Have no regard for his appearance or stature. . . . God doesn't look at things like humans do. Humans see only what is visible to the eyes, but the LORD sees into the heart" (16:7). Samuel himself had already delivered that message on God's behalf to Saul in announcing his descendants would not rule after him (13:14, footnote—"a man after his own heart"), but apparently Samuel needed to be reminded.

And Jesse needed to be reminded that he had another son. After Samuel had worked his way down the line assembled in front of him, saying that each in turn was not the one God had chosen, he asked Jesse, "Is that all of your boys?" Jesse replied that the youngest, David, was off tending the sheep. It hadn't occurred to him that Samuel could have any interest in him. But David was the one God had chosen, and he was the one Samuel "anointed . . . right there in front of his brothers" (16:13).

Paul Alludes to David

During his struggle with opponents in Corinth who emphasized a "theology of glory" in contrast to his "theology of the cross," Paul appears to make a very subtle allusion to God's reason for selecting David. Paul's opponents seemed to be bothered by Paul's emphasis on his own experiences of suffering in relationship to the gospel. He encouraged them to reject cultural notions about power and prestige: "we are giving you an opportunity to be proud of us so that you could answer those who take pride in superficial appearance, and not in what is in the heart" (2 Corinthians 5:12). Paul was able to stay true to his mission despite opposition both outside and within the church because his heart was attuned to God's purposes.

Carefully notice what is not said in this story. Samuel knows why he has come to Jesse's home in Bethlehem (16:1), but everyone else knows only that God has "chosen" David and that Samuel has anointed him. But for what has David been chosen and anointed? Obviously it wasn't apparent to everyone that it was to be king, otherwise the cover story to protect Samuel from execution for treason (see 16:2-3) would never have worked. Did David know from that moment that he would be king? All we are told explicitly is, "The LORD's spirit came over David from that point forward" (16:13b). Perhaps as Mary would do centuries later, he "committed these things to memory and considered them carefully" (literally, "kept them in her heart," Luke 2:19). Whatever the case, something of the nature of David's own heart must be seen in the fact that he didn't make a show of the fact that he was God's chosen and anointed, apparently not even to his older brothers (contrast young Joseph in Genesis 37:1-11).

David Arrives at the Royal Court (1 Samuel 16:14–18:6)

So deep did the division between Saul and David eventually become that, over time, people could not even agree on how David came to be at the court. There are two quite different accounts, the strongest correlation between the two being that each places Saul in a very negative light and David in a very positive one.

Indeed, the first story (16:14-23) draws a striking contrast between them. We have just seen that after David was anointed by Samuel "the LORD's spirit came over" him. Only seven words later (five in the Hebrew text), we are told, "the LORD's spirit *had departed* from Saul, and an evil spirit from the LORD tormented him" (16:14, emphasis added). In order to provide some comfort for Saul, who is presented as descending into madness, his advisors recommend that "one of Jesse's sons" be brought to the court. Already, a royal advisor knows David as "a good musician...a strong man and heroic, a warrior who speaks well and is good-looking too. The LORD is with him" (16:18). In short, he is everything Saul once was but is no more—exactly the kind of person those who "see only what is visible to the eyes" would want at the royal court. Everything goes exactly as planned. David's music calms Saul in his times of torment. Saul grows to like (and presumably rely on) David so much that he becomes his armor-bearer.

About the Scripture

The Heavenly Court

As Christians reading the Old Testament, we need to be careful that we do not read back into it theological ideas that only developed later. Thus, we should not equate expressions like "the LORD's spirit" with trinitarian teaching about "the Holy Spirit." By the same token, we should not take a statement like "an evil spirit from the LORD" to mean that God sends demons to torment people. In both expressions, the Old Testament is drawing on an image of a heavenly court in which spiritual beings gather before God's throne and are sent as emissaries to accomplish God's purposes. Some bring comfort, others judgment. The classic example of this imagery is found in Job 1:6–2:10, where even "the Adversary" (Hebrew, *has-satan*) is one of the "divine beings" serving an assigned task within God's court.

Then comes the second story—David and Goliath (17:1–18:5). This story is well known even to children (at least in versions as carefully expunged of such gory details as chopping off heads and parading them around [17:51, 54, and 57] as any Disney retelling of a Grimm's fairy tale).

What is often overlooked, however, is that it doesn't fit at all with the earlier story. If David is already known to be a "heroic warrior," why isn't he among the troops to begin with? The comic scene of the boy swallowed in the king's unfamiliar armor (17:38-39) doesn't fit with the information that David was Saul's armor-bearer.

Even if the details don't square between the two stories, the overall tone is just the same. Saul has so failed as king that he requires David to save him—whether from his madness or from Goliath. When David does so, Saul keeps him in service at the court (16:21; 18:2). And in both instances, David assumes his role as a faithful servant of the king even though Samuel has already anointed him as God's chosen leader for Israel. He makes no attempt to usurp the throne or even to challenge Saul's fitness to reign.

For Saul, Friendship Turns to Enmity (1 Samuel 18:7–26:25)

Despite David's loyalty, it doesn't take long before Saul becomes jealous of his popularity with the people and uneasy about his ability to retain his position as king (18:8). He attempts to rid himself of his rival by ordering David to lead military campaigns from which Saul is confident he will never return (a lesson in court intrigue, we will see, that David apparently never forgot; 2 Samuel 11:14-21). When such indirect means failed, Saul ordered Jonathan to kill David (1 Samuel 19:1).

Rather than carry out his father's order, Jonathan instead warned David to go into hiding so that he could try to convince Saul of his loyalty. At least initially Jonathan succeeded (19:4-7), but it didn't last. Saul himself tried to kill David with a spear, and when he failed, he ordered that his guard seize David in order that he might be executed. But this time, Saul's efforts were thwarted by two of his children. His daughter Michal, who was also David's wife, warned David to flee in the night. And once again Jonathan tried to intercede on David's behalf, but Saul even attacked him because of his allegiance to David (20:30-33). Convinced of his father's intention to kill David, Jonathan secretly warned David not to return to the court (20:35-42).

What follows in Chapters 21–26 of First Samuel is a series of stories of Saul's repeated attempts to use his army to locate and kill David. Rather than use his own troops against Saul, David himself takes advantage of opportunities to lead raids against Israel's Philistine enemies. Among the stories in this series are two accounts (in Chapters 24 and 26 respectively) of incidents when David had opportunity to kill Saul but refused to take it, although in each instance he made sure that both Saul and everyone else knew about it.

In the first instance, David was able to cut away a portion of Saul's robe as he was relieving himself in the darkness of a cave (24:1-7). In the second, David was able to make off with both Saul's spear and his water jug that were at his side while he slept in the very midst of his troops (26:7-12). Both times, David then called out to Saul and his troops, displaying his trophies as proof that he could have displayed Saul's head before them (as he had Goliath's before). But for David, Saul was still "the LORD's anointed" and for that reason, he would not harm him (24:6; 26:9).

As readers of these stories, we cannot help but notice the contrast between David's actions toward Saul as "the LORD's anointed" and Saul's actions against David who was also "the LORD's anointed." David's own troops looked at the circumstances in that cave and that night as Saul slept and saw them as God-given opportunities to be rid of his enemy. But David was more concerned about his own actions in those moments than Saul's actions in the past. We are told that David even "felt horrible that he had cut off a corner of Saul's robe" (24:5). He couldn't control what Saul might do, but he would continue to act responsibly himself.

For David, Loyalty Was Foremost (1 Samuel 27–31)

To bring an end to the repeated skirmishes with Saul's forces, David finally withdrew into the lower hill country that was controlled by the Philistines (27:1-4). While he was there, he found a way to be of service both to Achish, the Philistine who ruled the region, and to his own people in Israel by carrying out raids against several tribal groups in the southern regions spreading into Shur (the Sinai peninsula). So strong was David's reputation for loyalty that Achish was prepared to include David and his troops among the Philistine forces assembled at Aphek for a strike against Saul, but the other Philistine commanders would have no part of it (29:1-11).

David's loyalty extended not only to those he considered his superiors. It was also apparent in his actions toward his troops. After being discharged by Achish, he returned to his base at Ziklag to find that the Amalekites had raided the town while he and his troops had been away. They had taken every inhabitant as captives and burned the structures to the ground. David rallied all six hundred of his troops, but as they pursued the Amalekites, some two hundred of them were forced to create a base at Besor because they were too exhausted to continue.

Once David's force overtook the raiders and defeated them, "rescu[ing] everything that the Amalekites had taken" (30:18), those who had fought with David declared all the sheep, cattle, and other livestock to be "David's plunder" and were particularly opposed to sharing it with those who had stayed back at the base in Besor. But David rejected that plan: "The share of those who went into battle and the share of those who stayed with the supplies will be divided equally" (30:24). Beyond that, he also sent portions of the spoils to the inhabitants of villages and towns within Judah where David and his men and spent time during Saul's pursuit of them.

This approach by David was not simply a response to their years of loyalty to him. From the moment he left Saul's court, he had been as concerned for others as he was for his own well-being. When David had requested supplies from the priest Ahimelech, he procured bread not only for himself but also for those who were going to rendezvous with him (21:1-6). And he assured Ahimelech that both he and his men had maintained their religious responsibilities even in the midst of the conflict.

Across the Testaments

Jesus Uses David as an Illustration

Despite the popularity of several of the stories about David's rise as Israel's king, especially his encounter with Goliath, there are actually very few references to the second half of First Samuel in the New Testament. In fact, aside from appearances in genealogies or similar lists or allusions like that in 2 Corinthians 5:12, 1 Samuel 21:1-6 is the only passage from these chapters that figures prominently at all.

Jesus uses this story in response to those who were upset that his disciples had gleaned heads of wheat on the Sabbath (Mark 2:23-28). There were two relevant points about David's actions from Jesus' perspective. First, strictly speaking, David's taking of the bread was a violation of religious practice because he took "the bread of the presence, which only the priests were allowed to eat." Second, David took the bread not only for himself but also shared it with those who were with him. For Jesus, this action illustrated the principle that religious practice exists to serve the legitimate needs of people; people do not exist to serve the needs of religious practice. "The Sabbath was created for humans; humans weren't created for the Sabbath."

Live the Story

Some of the greatest challenges in life come when the actions of others seem to deny us those things that, by all accounts, would seem to be rightfully ours. It is only natural in such situations to want to strike out and take what has been promised to us. But as the Scriptures remind us, what seems "natural" to us as we await the full revelation of what it means for us to be God's sons and daughters (see Romans 8:18-25) isn't always what is faithful in either our relationship with God or with others.

What specific things might you be able to do that would maintain faithfulness with others who may have already broken faith with you? Think about not only circumstances within your immediate network of family and friends, but in broader networks of your community, the nation, and the world (even "the whole creation" itself, as Romans 8:19 reminds us). Certainly in those broader networks there will be things beyond your control, but what things *can* you do that would make some difference? Where in your relationship with God can you find the strength you need to do these things?

3.

The Challenge of Blessings

2 Samuel 1–10

Claim Your Story

What would you do if you won the lottery or through some other serendipitous means suddenly came into more wealth than you really knew what to do with? Most of us would probably quit our jobs, even if we kept doing some of the things in our occupations that we truly enjoy. (That's what some retirees do, isn't it?) Certainly we would invest some of it to be sure we will be taken care of as we grow older. We would pay off any debts we have, purchase a few of the things we really enjoy (or things that help us do the things we enjoy), and probably give nice gifts to family members.

And then what? Well, we might follow the pattern of philanthropists and endow some projects that would benefit people we don't even know. Maybe fund scholarships at the ol' alma mater or establish a medical research center to work on a cure for some dread disease.

How many of us, however, would ever think to look for ways that we could use our good fortune to benefit those who had wronged us in the past? Would the thought even cross our minds? Would it strike many folks as crazy?

When have you seen someone benefit from the generosity of an opponent? When has that happened to you? When have you sought to bring good to someone who has wronged you?

Enter the Bible Story

Even within the narrative flow of First and Second Samuel, there is a case to be made that David didn't exactly "win the lottery." To be sure, the story about how he came to be chosen by God from among Jesse's sons and anointed by Samuel to become king of Israel (1 Samuel 16:1-13) is a bit like winning the lottery. But the years when he was being pursued by Saul's forces, when he was engaged in raids against Israel's enemies, were long and hard. Despite the poetic turns of phrase sometimes used (like in 2 Samuel 7:8), David didn't go straight from tending sheep to being the shepherd and leader of Israel. Yet it can certainly be said that there was no reasonable path by which the youngest boy of eight brothers tending his father's flock could have expected to become a king.

As Second Samuel opens following the death of Saul and Jonathan in battle at Mount Gilboa (recounted in 1 Samuel 31), it still is not certain that David will in fact become king. David had built a strong reputation both among his own tribe of Judah and across the other tribes of Israel. But Saul had an heir, his son Ishbosheth, and there were those in the military under Abner's leadership who were loyal to Saul. David had not yet even returned from his refuge in the Philistine foothills to the west of the hill country of Judah.

David Responds to Saul's Death (2 Samuel 1)

The details of Saul's death as reported by the narrator of the story in 1 Samuel 31:1-6 and in the report David received from one who had escaped the battle (2 Samuel 1:6-10) don't exactly jibe. Keeping in mind that originally, these stories flowed seamlessly within a single book of Samuel without even the chapter and verse breaks added centuries later, the discrepancies were hardly lost on either the author or the early readers. Perhaps the differences are to be attributed to what we call "the fog of war"; but then again, maybe we are to conclude that other motivations were at play.

According to the narrator of Samuel, Saul's sons Jonathan, Abinadab, and Malchishua were killed when the Philistines overtook Saul's routed army on the slopes of Mount Gilboa. As the focus of the Philistine attack shifted to the segment of Saul's forces under his direct command, Saul was badly wounded by the archers in advance of the infantry attack. Fearing that he would be captured and tortured, Saul commanded his armor-bearer to dispatch him with his sword. When the armor-bearer, in terror, refused to carry out the order, Saul ended his own life by impaling himself upon his sword. The armor-bearer then took his own life in the same manner and died with his king.

The initial details David received were not that different. The young Amalekite told him that he came upon Saul in convulsions caused by previously received wounds as mounted Philistine forces were closing in for the final attack. Saul asked that young man (not his armor-bearer) to kill him before the Philistines could finish him, and the young man fulfilled the request. He then took Saul's crown and bracelet, and brought them to David.

If the young man had simply come upon the impaled body of Saul on the battlefield and decided to take the crown as spoils, bringing it to David in hopes of currying his favor for having killed his enemy, then the scheme was a miserable failure. Rather than rewarding the Amalekite, David ordered him summarily executed since by his account he had "killed the LORD's anointed" (1:16). David lamented rather than rejoiced at Saul's death. It was the first sign that David would not seek vengeance on Saul's family now that Saul himself was dead. Indeed, David did not even presume to declare himself king.

David provides a model for us here of seeing our lives in a broader context. It would be easy for anyone who had shared such experiences of hardship at the hands of others to see in the blessings of deliverance also the opportunities for retribution. As we gain, we may be driven to use that position of strength to take even more from those who have deprived us in the past. But such cycles of vengeance will consume those who are drawn into them. The only way to break free is to multiply the good things that come into our lives by using them to do good for others.

Israel Descends Into Civil War (2 Samuel 2–4)

It was only "some time later" (2:1) that David asked God whether he should leave his refuge and return to his tribal homeland of Judah. Almost immediately, the clans of Judah gathered at Hebron "and anointed David king over the house of Judah" (2:4)—over their single tribe. Yet his approach toward the remaining tribes of Israel remained rather low-key. Once established in Judah, he sent word to the city of Jabesh-gilead—well within the territory of the northern tribes—commending them for their loyalty to Saul in recovering his body from the battlefield and also announcing that he was now king over Judah. It was a gesture, however, that could not have gone unnoticed by Ishbosheth, who ruled over the other tribes from Mahanaim that was also in Gilead.

David and Ishbosheth may have been guardedly keeping their distance from one another, but their respective military leaders were not. Abner led Ishbosheth's forces on an excursion out of Gilead and back to Gibeon in the hill country of Benjamin—right on Judah's northern frontier. Joab led David's forces north and confronted them. As the armies faced one another, Abner called for a "contest" between representatives from Benjamin and Judah (2:14). As the footnote explains, there is some uncertainty about the precise meaning of "contest." Was this simply an opportunity to "play" and "compete" against one another in some kind of sport or was it meant to be a "contest" of champions where prime warriors from each camp squared off against one another in lieu of a full-fledged battle (as Goliath had challenged Saul's army in the Elah Valley; 1 Samuel 17:4-10)? Whatever the intent, at the end of the "contest" every participant from both sides lay dead in the field. Joab's forces drove Abner's from the field in the battle that ensued, but Abner killed Joab's brother Asahel during the pursuit. As the narrator summarizes, "The war between Saul's house and David's house was long and drawn out. David kept getting stronger, while Saul's house kept getting weaker" (2 Samuel 3:1).

About the Scripture

Ishbosheth's Seat of Power

That Abner established Ishbosheth's seat of power in Mahanaim may be an indication of his weakness relative to both David and the Philistines. Mahanaim was on the eastern side of the Jordan rift valley (in the modern state of Jordan), far removed from the Philistine cities along the Mediterranean coast and the western foothills and from David in the mountainous hill country of Judah. In contrast, Saul had maintained his seat of power in Gibeah, within the tribal allotment of his own tribe of Benjamin and immediately north of Judah in the hill country.

Eventually Abner and Ishbosheth would sue for peace, with Abner promising to bring all the forces of Israel's tribes into allegiance with David under Abner's command (3:17-19). When Joab learned of the deal, he assassinated Abner in retaliation for his brother Asahel's death. David was furious with Joab and equally furious with those who sought to gain his favor by assassinating Ishbosheth as he slept (4:1-12). David had become king of all Israel, but he insisted that the means by which it had come about had left him "weak" (3:39a).

Part of what set David apart from those around him was that he recognized that using power *against* others rather than *for* others served to diminish one's self along with those against whom the power is directed. We cannot secure good things for ourselves through attacks on others. As the old saying goes, live long enough by "an eye for an eye," and soon the whole world will be blind. Blessings and life come when they are shared by all and not when they are denied to some so they can be hoarded by others.

David Consolidates His Rule (2 Samuel 5–8)

Representatives from all the tribes traveled to Hebron to form a covenant with David and thereby bring to fulfillment the promise they acknowledged that God had made to him: "You will shepherd my people Israel, and you will be Israel's leader" (5:2).

Across the Testaments

Matthew Quotes Second Samuel

One of the features of the birth narrative in Matthew's Gospel is the evangelist's use of "fulfillment quotations." At several points along the way, he inserts a comment like, "this took place so that what the Lord had spoken through the prophet would be fulfilled" (Matthew 1:22 is the first example). In conjunction with the story that Jesus was born in Bethlehem, the evangelist, in Matthew 2:6, combines a quotation from Micah 5:2 about Bethlehem with the statement about David in 2 Samuel 5:2 that he would "shepherd my people Israel." This combination of quotations from Micah and Second Samuel can help us understand how the evangelist conceived of these "fulfillments." Rather than prophets predicting, centuries in advance, specific details exclusively about Jesus, the evangelist sees in the coming of Jesus the culmination of things God had already begun. David, the shepherd king, had indeed led God's people Israel, and now in Jesus, God would shepherd "disciples of all nations" (see Matthew 28:19-20).

David did specific things to consolidate his rule in Israel, each in response to a particular strain on the unity of the people. First, David worked to bring an end to the endless raids and incursions that the Israelites had suffered from peoples both along their borders (most notably, the Philistines; 5:17-25) and within their tribal regions. The most important example of the latter was the capture of the Jebusite fortress on Zion in Jerusalem (5:6-10). By relocating his seat of governance to Jerusalem, David was able to place it in a city that had not previously been under the control of any particular tribe while at the same time keeping it within the general region of Judah, his own ancestral tribe. To appreciate the politics of that action, recall how the capital of the United States was ultimately located in a special district (the District of Columbia) so that no state would be the seat of the national government. Second, David further legitimated both his new seat of government and his rule by transferring "the LORD's chest" (the ark of the covenant) to Jerusalem and permanently housing it within a tent that he had pitched for it (6:1-19).

At long last, "the king was settled in his palace and the LORD had given him rest from all his surrounding enemies" (7:1). David summoned the prophet Nathan to consult about his plans for what he wanted to do next. "Look! I'm living in a cedar palace, but God's chest is housed in a tent!" (7:2). It was time to share his blessings with others. Even before he could spell out his intentions, Nathan assured him, "Go ahead and do whatever you are thinking, because the LORD is with you" (7:3).

But as Nathan slept that night, God directed him to go back and tell David, "Not so fast," though not in those words. The actual message is a marvel of language: It plays on a number of different uses of the Hebrew word *beth*, which as the footnote at 7:1 points out can have a range of meanings from "house," to "temple," to "palace," to "family," to "dynasty." Does David wish to build a *beth* ("temple") for God because his own *beth* ("palace") is so luxurious? Instead, God will transform David's *beth* ("family") into a *beth* ("dynasty") that will rule over Israel forever.

After Nathan delivers the oracle to David the next day, David offers a prayer every bit as eloquent in extolling God as the source of blessing both David himself and all of Israel (7:18-29). It is God alone who had brought David to his place as king of Israel. It is only God who can possibly secure that role for him and his family both now and into the future. God alone has brought blessing and greatness to Israel by delivering Israel from Egypt and from their enemies.

David Shows "Faithful Love" to Mephibosheth (2 Samuel 9)

Unable to respond to the blessings in his life by building a house/temple for God, David once more turns his attention to the house/family of Saul. Despite all the years that Saul sought to have him killed, despite the years of civil war between his forces and those of Ishbosheth, David nonetheless asked, "Is there anyone from Saul's family still alive that I could show faithful love for Jonathan's sake?" (9:1).

"Faithful Love"

The Hebrew word translated by the expression "faithful love," as in 2 Samuel 9:1, is *chesed*. Scholars have vigorously debated its nuances. Some stress the commitments, bonds, and obligations that love places upon us. Others emphasize the mercy and grace of love that is truly unconditional. Both these things are true of the most profound expressions of love, but the two strands can sometimes come into conflict. Sometimes the loving thing to do is to hold people accountable for their actions, make them fulfill their obligations rather than mercifully excusing every destructive act. We will look at this tension (if not the specific word *chesed*) more fully in the next chapter.

From Ziba, a servant of Saul's household, David learned about Jonathan's only surviving son, Mephibosheth. He was only five years old when his father died on Mount Gilboa. As those who cared for him tried to get him to safety, he had suffered an accident that had left him crippled in both feet (4:4). David directed that Mephibosheth be brought to Jerusalem and become a part of the royal household. Ziba was to maintain Saul's estate for the benefit of Saul's family and the other remaining servants of Saul's household. But David would directly show to Mephibosheth the "faithful love" that would otherwise have been given to his father Jonathan, and even to his grandfather Saul.

There is a passing phrase in this story that quietly marks how different an example David provides for us from our usual experience. After Mephibosheth confirms his identity, David's very next words to him are, "Don't be afraid" (9:7). What is thinly veiled behind those words is no doubt Mephibosheth's expectation that the final move in David's plan to consolidate his role as Israel's king would be to assassinate the last possible heir to Saul's throne and that David's claim of initiating the search from a desire to show "faithful love" was only a deceitful ruse. Imagine Mephibosheth's relief, then, when David proved to be as good as his word.

David had obtained all the good things in life that come from being the king. He had used them to provide for himself and his family. Then he had moved beyond his own circle of relationships. He worked to extend the blessings of security and prosperity beyond his own family, beyond his own tribe, to all the people of Israel. But then he did the truly unexpected thing: He searched out opportunities to share these blessings even with those who had been his enemies. It was that final move, perhaps more than all the others, that demonstrated why he was "*a man who shares [God's] desires*" (Acts 13:22).

Live the Story

The probability that anyone reading this study will ever live a royal lifestyle like David is essentially nil. We are not likely to "win the lottery" in either a literal sense or figuratively because our own efforts pay off to an unimaginable degree. But if we don't compare ourselves to the likes of David in Scripture or Warren Buffett and his ilk in *The Wall Street Journal*, look at how we rank next to most of the world's current population: Just by the simple serendipity of being born at this time into this culture we have been unimaginably blessed.

The issue, then, is what are we going to do with whatever degree of blessing we have received? Are we going to hold it tightly for ourselves and for our closest family members, whether out of worry that it might not last or because of a sense that we've earned or are otherwise entitled to it? Or, can we see that the things that we have are not solely for our own benefit but are also to be shared for the benefit of community—even with those who may have wronged us in the past?

And what, specifically, should we do as a result of that insight?

4.

Accountable Forgiveness

2 Samuel 11–24

Claim Your Story

"Just forgive and forget." There are those for whom that statement represents the highest expression of what grace is all about. To forgive and to forget is to reset a damaged relationship as if nothing had ever happened to damage it. After all, we can't help but question the sincerity of anyone who would say, "I forgive you, but I'll never forget."

Certainly, there are times when forgetfulness is an intrinsic part of forgiveness. Yet there are also times when forgiveness may be necessary to restore the relationship but forgetting simply is not possible—times when the actions that caused the break in the relationship to begin with continue to have consequences that forgiveness just can't erase. Granting forgiveness to the perpetrator may be essential to the healing of those who have lost a loved one to a murder or even the reckless acts of another who was, say, driving while intoxicated. But forgiveness cannot bring people back to life, and we wouldn't want it to erase the memories of them as if they had never lived. There are even times when, while divine forgiveness can fully restore our relationship with God, it cannot spare us from the consequences of our actions.

When have you found it difficult or nearly impossible to forgive someone for something done to you or a loved one? If you did forgive that person, how did it change you? If you have not forgiven that person, how are you affected?

What hard things have occurred in your life or your family that may be the consequence, directly or indirectly, of a bad decision or wrongdoing on your part? What role has God's forgiveness played in your dealing with those consequences?

When has someone's forgiveness of you helped you recover your inner peace?

Enter the Bible Story

To this point in First and Second Samuel, David has been the great hero. As a military leader, his exploits were literally the stuff of legend (Goliath) and song: "Saul has killed his thousands, but David has killed his tens of thousands" (1 Samuel 18:7)—a song so well known that even Israel's enemies the Philistines could sing along (1 Samuel 21:11; 29:5). As a political leader, he worked to build support across all the tribes (2 Samuel 2:1, 7; 5:1-4) rather than asserting a right to be king based solely on having been anointed by Samuel. He shrewdly located his seat of government in Jerusalem, a town he had made his own by taking it from the Jebusites but still within his ancestral tribe of Judah's sphere of influence (2 Samuel 5:6-10). As a spiritual leader, he was a psalmist with extraordinary abilities to soothe troubled spirits (1 Samuel 16:14-21). He understood the role the worship of God could play in uniting the people and was unafraid to display his own religious zeal before the people (2 Samuel 6:12b-15). As a benefactor, his great desire was to build a temple for God (2 Samuel 7), and he went to great lengths to show "faithful love" to Saul's family despite all that had transpired between them (2 Samuel 9).

All that was about to change.

David and Bathsheba (2 Samuel 11–12)

The turn in David's story begins with marvelous literary artistry. "In the spring, when kings go off to war," the narrator tells us, "David sent Joab...and all the Israelites" into battle against the Ammonites at Rabbah. *"But David remained in Jerusalem"* (11:1, emphasis added). The mighty warrior king was not where he should have been, and the consequences unleashed by that fact would nearly destroy David and his family.

As David was enjoying the evening views of his city from his palace roof, the thing that caught his eye the most was a beautiful woman bathing on another rooftop. He inquired as to who she was and was told it was "Eliam's daughter Bathsheba, the wife of Uriah the Hittite" (11:3). Now, in that brief statement associating Bathsheba with two men should have been enough to stop David in his tracks. She was the daughter of Eliam, one of David's most trusted warriors (23:34), and thus also the grand-daughter of Ahithophel, one of the most influential men in all of Israel (16:23). She was the wife of Uriah the Hittite, one of the mercenary leaders in David's army that was at that very moment conducting the siege he had ordered. So, what was David thinking?

Well, the narrator leaves little doubt about what he was thinking: David sent for Bathsheba, and "he had sex with her." Moreover, the narrator removes any suspense about what will happen next by the parenthetical notice, "Now she had been purifying herself after her monthly period" (11:4). Might there have been something about the manner that she was bathing on that rooftop that should have signaled that information to David as well? Was that yet another indication of just how reckless David was being? However that may be, Bathsheba's report to David is as simple and direct as the narrator's report of David's actions: "I'm pregnant" (11:5).

David first tries to cover up his wrongdoing. He orders Uriah back from the front under the guise of needing a report on the siege progress. Once back in Jerusalem, David sends him to enjoy all the pleasures of his home, but Uriah proves himself more a man of duty than David: "My master Joab and my master's troops are camping in the open field. How could I go home and eat, drink, and have sex with my wife?" (11:11; remember, David was well aware of the military custom of abstinence during campaigns, 1 Samuel 21:4-5). When the cover-up failed, David borrowed a tactic that Saul had once tried against him (see 1 Samuel 18:25-27) by sending Uriah on a military mission that was doomed to fail. This time the tactic worked, and word came back from the front: "*Your servant* Uriah the Hittite is dead" (2 Samuel 11:24, emphasis added). The way was now clear for Bathsheba to become David's wife, and she "bore him a son."

In one of the most dramatic scenes in all of Scripture, God sends David's court prophet Nathan to confront him. He tells David a story about a rich man who took the only ewe lamb owned by a man so poor that the ewe was a key to sustaining his family. Rather than diminish his own vast flocks by even one sheep, the rich man had killed the lamb and offered it as hospitality extended to a traveler. David was furious at such a violation of all human decency: "As surely as the LORD lives, the one who did this is demonic!" (12:5). Not realizing that Nathan's story is a parable rather than an actual happening, David orders that restitution be made seven-times over.

"You are that man!" Nathan declared (12:7). David was the one who was "rich" with God's blessings but had stolen the blessings and even the life of another man. Perhaps you can make restitution by substituting one ewe with even more livestock, but there was no bringing Uriah back from the dead. If there could be no restitution, there would certainly be consequences: "the sword will never leave your own house" (12:10).

David exclaimed, "I've sinned against the LORD!" (12:13). And Nathan all but shouts back, "The LORD has removed your sin," but the consequences still remain—beginning with the death of the child born of David's imposition of himself on Bathsheba. When the newborn became ill, David began to fast and pray that God would heal him. His grief was so severe as the baby struggled with the illness that David's servants were afraid to bring him the news a week later that the child was dead. To their amazement, once David learned of the boy's death, he resumed his normal routine, not even participating in the customary mourning rituals. When asked about his behavior, David explained that as long as the child still lived there was some hope that God might mercifully heal him. Now that he was dead, that hope was gone. His relationship with both Bathsheba and God would move forward. She gave birth to their second son whom he named Solomon, and "the LORD loved him" (12:24). But David would only be restored to his first son in the grave (12:23).

The story of David's relationship with Bathsheba brings together some of humanity's most grievous sins: deception, sexual infidelity, murder. It is also a story of the ready availability of divine grace. There is neither elaborate ritual of penance on David's part nor a moment's hesitation on

The Women in Jesus' Genealogy

In Jesus' genealogy at the beginning of Matthew, Solomon is listed as the son of David from whom Jesus is descended. What is most striking, however, is that the evangelist identifies Solomon's mother as "the wife of Uriah" (Matthew 1:6). Thus, Bathsheba somewhat anonymously joins only four other women in the genealogy: Tamar, Rahab, Ruth, and Jesus' own mother, Mary. All these women share in common that they lived under a cloud of sexual suspicion. Both Tamar (Genesis 38) and Ruth (Ruth 3–4) not only gave birth to their sons through the unusual circumstances of levirate marriage, but sexual seduction figures prominently in their stories. Rahab was the prostitute who hid the spies in Jericho (Joshua 2:1-21). And of course, Mary was pregnant with Jesus before she was married to Joseph.

Commentators on Matthew differ in their explanations for why the evangelist mentions only these women. In conjunction with the story of David and Bathsheba, we can certainly see that one aspect is that God works to bring redemption through those places in human life where it is most needed.

Nathan's in pronouncing God's forgiveness. The story drives home the point, however, that while forgiveness makes possible renewed relationship, it cannot always remove the consequences of acts that require forgiveness. And as the next act in David's story will make clear, pretending that forgiveness must spare the one forgiven all consequences can be more destructive to relationships than withholding forgiveness in the first place.

The Price for David's Sin (2 Samuel 14–24)

Let's just come right out and say it: Aside from a moving psalm of praise to the God who is our faithful deliverer in Chapter 22, there is nothing fit for children in the second half of Second Samuel. All the elements of human evil on display in the David and Bathsheba episode erupt on an ever larger scale. Sexual infidelity gives way to incestuous rape. Arranging the circumstances of another's certain death gives way to direct murder. Deceit as a tool to cover up past wrongdoing gives way to deception for purposes of committing rape and murder. And this tortured path is paved by a misguided sense of love that refuses to hold people accountable for their actions.

The carnage began when Amnon fell in love with his half sister, Tamar. Because they were both David's children by different wives, Amnon knew that it would never be possible for them to be together. At the prompting of a friend within the family (a cousin, the son of one of his father's brothers; 13:3), Amnon carried out a plot to rape her (13:6-18). "When King David heard about all this he got very angry, but he refused to punish his son Amnon because he loved him as his oldest child" (13:21). But Tamar's full-brother Absalom neither forgave nor forgot what Amnon had done to his sister.

For no less than two years, Absalom plotted his revenge. Just as Amnon had used David to arrange Tamar's presence in his chambers for the rape (13:6-8), so Absalom used David to help bring Amnon to his banqueting hall (13:23-27). Once Amnon was "happy with wine" (13:28), Absalom gave the signal and his servants murdered Amnon. David was grief-stricken; but over time, as Absalom stayed away from the court, "the king's desire to go out after Absalom faded away because he had gotten over Amnon's death" (13:39). Even when Joab believed he had convinced David to hold Absalom accountable for what he had done (14:1-23), David did little more than place him under house arrest for about two years. When Absalom finally received an audience before his father (prompted by an act of arson against Joab; 14:29-32), "the king kissed Absalom" (14:33).

Having quite literally gotten away with murder, Absalom began sowing the seeds for his rebellion. For a period of four years, Absalom intercepted as many petitioners to the royal court as he could and assured them, "No doubt your claims are correct and valid, but the king won't listen to you. If only I were made a judge in the land . . . I would give them justice" (15:3-4). Finally, and with the king's blessing (15:9), Absalom went to Hebron. Once there, he sent out the word, "Absalom has become king in Hebron!" (15:10), and many people rallied to him.

David was forced to flee Jerusalem and take refuge on the eastern side of the Jordan Valley, but he took care to leave people within the city whom he could trust.

After Absalom returned to Jerusalem from Hebron, he sought the advice of Ahithophel, who had been one of David's trusted advisors, regarding how he might consolidate his claim to the throne. Ahithophel advised Absalom to demonstrate that he had completely broken with his father by having "sex with your father's secondary wives." When Absalom carried out that advice on a rooftop "in plain sight before all Israel" (16:21-22), not only did Ahithophel avenge his honor for what David had done with his granddaughter Bathsheba, but Nathan's oracle was literally fulfilled as well (see 12:11-12).

David, however, refused to disavow his son even as the battle lines were forming between his forces and Absalom's. The final orders David gave to his commanders as they prepared for the engagement were, "For my sake, protect my boy Absalom" (18:5). It was an order that Joab refused to carry out. Some twenty thousand men died in the battle, including Absalom. He had become entangled in the branches of an oak tree as he left the battle. When Joab received the report, he and his troops killed Absalom where he hung rather than return him to his father.

The only news David wanted to hear from the front was the fate of his son. Upon learning that he was dead, David cried out, "Oh, my son Absalom! . . . If only I had died instead of you! Oh, Absalom, my son! My son!" (18:33). Joab was furious. "Today you have humiliated all your servants who have saved your life today. . . by loving those who hate you and hating those who love you! Today you have announced that the commanders and their soldiers are nothing to you, because I know that if Absalom were alive today and the rest of us dead, that would be perfectly fine with you!" (19:5-6). David's only hope of maintaining his troops' loyalty and retaining the kingdom, Joab told him, would be by leaving his mourning aside and going out to greet them.

David did as Joab urged and was able to regain the allegiance of the tribes, if not the unity among them. Tensions between Judah and the other tribes would soon lead to yet another rebellion, this time led by a "despicable man" named Sheba under the rallying cry, "We don't care about David! We have no stake in Jesse's son! Go back to your homes, Israel!" (20:1). Joab's forces put down the rebellion in relatively short order, but the split between Judah and the other tribes foreshadowed events to come a generation later.

It would appear from David's dealings with both his sons Amnon and Absalom that perhaps he had drawn the wrong lesson when Nathan so quickly offered the assurance, "The LORD has removed your sin," in the wake of his murderous wrongdoing with Bathsheba. Perhaps David was so overcome with grief at the loss of the first child born to him and Bathsheba that he couldn't face the possible loss of other sons. Yet how he quickly put aside his grief at the time of that child's death makes that explanation seem unlikely.

We are probably better off learning from David's mistake than trying to psychoanalyze the reasons for it. David himself had been forgiven by God, but also held accountable for his actions. David had extended only unconditional love to Amnon and Absalom, when what they needed was a love strong enough to also hold them accountable for their actions. Had he loved them enough to both forgive and to correct them, then perhaps both his family and all of Israel could have been spared the deadly consequences of their increasingly violent acts.

Live the Story

Think about those places in your life where your relationships are damaged and in need of forgiveness—both those where you were the one harmed, and those where it was your actions that caused the break. In which case is it harder to see that forgiveness and acceptance of painful consequences sometimes go hand in hand? Can you remember times when your eagerness to restore a relationship led you to offer the cheap forgiveness that sheltered someone from consequences but in the process, denied the opportunity needed to grow and mature? Have there been times when you've been unable to accept that you yourself have truly been forgiven because the one you had wronged did not spare you the consequences of what you had done?

Some recovery programs for addictive behaviors are founded on the essential relationship between giving/receiving forgiveness and requiring/accepting responsibility. They recognize that in a deep sense, neither is possible without the other. Many also insist that our ability to accomplish this balance in our human relationships is only possible once we have accepted that God's forgiveness is also not an escape hatch from consequences. It may be "tough love," but it is also genuine forgiveness.

What action does this biblical story call for in your life?

5.

Solomon—The Good, the Bad, and the Ugly

1 Kings 1–11

Claim Your Story

Nashville, Tennessee, takes pride in being known as "the Athens of the South." Reflecting that identity, the city built a full-scale replica of the Parthenon in Athens, Greece, for the Tennessee state centennial exposition in 1897. That temporary structure was replaced by a permanent one in the 1920s. During the 1980s, an almost 42-foot tall statue of Pallas Athena was installed in the building, roughly coinciding with the construction of the Sri Ganesha Temple elsewhere in the city with its many images of the elephant-headed deity of Hinduism. Some at the time wondered how this city in the Bible belt was becoming a "city of idols."

The idea that people might actually worship the goddess Athena during a visit to Nashville's Parthenon art museum is admittedly far-fetched, as was any concern that the Sri Ganesha Temple might lead to mass conversions to Hinduism among Tennesseans. No, as the title of the popular television show suggests, the idols that draw the loyalties of Americans tend to be success, fame, and wealth. And despite all the attention given to temples and foreign gods in the stories about Solomon, his greatest struggles were with the idolization of the same things that tempt us today.

What "things" threaten to derail your spiritual life?

Enter the Bible Story

In part because of his vaunted reputation for wisdom, and in part because of his role in the construction of the first Jerusalem Temple,

Solomon is often considered one of Israel's greatest kings. That he was also the last king of the so-called United Monarchy over all the tribes and didn't face the rivalry that existed between Saul and David or the rebellions that emerged in the last years of David's reign probably help as well. But consideration of the beginning and end of Solomon's reign may produce a more measured assessment. It was hardly certain that Solomon would succeed his father David on the throne, and his own policies did much to set the stage for the division of the kingdom when his son Rehoboam succeeded him.

Solomon's Accession to the Throne (1 Kings 1–2)

With a detail that's full significance will only later become apparent, First Kings opens with a brief story about how David's servants searched throughout Israel to find a beautiful young woman to attend to him in his old age and keep him warm in his bed. Abishag from Shunem was chosen, but the narrator insists "the king didn't have sex with her" (1:4). If, as seems possible, the story is intended to present a picture of an impotent king in more than one sense of the word, the events that unfold demonstrate that there was still some life left in David.

Adonijah, the son of David and Haggith, born while David reigned only over Judah from Hebron (2 Samuel 3:2-5), was apparently the next in line for the throne after Absalom—at least according to birth order. He began to position himself to succeed David by enlisting the support of Joab, Abiathar the priest, and other members of the court. Purposefully excluded, however, were Nathan, Benaiah (another of David's military commanders), and Solomon.

Nathan brought the news to Bathsheba that Adonijah was positioning himself to be king, and together they carefully orchestrated a plan to provoke David into declaring, in advance of his own death, Solomon as king. Along with Benaiah, they enlisted Zadok the priest in their plan as well. In the persons of Nathan, Benaiah, and Zadok, all three major leadership factions in Israel—the prophets, the military, and the priests—were aligned behind Solomon.

First, Bathsheba came to David, asking him to confirm his promise to her that Solomon would succeed him as king since "now... Adonijah has become king, and my master doesn't know about it" (1 Kings 1:18). Next, while Bathsheba was still with David, Nathan arrived and essentially asked David why he had confirmed Adonijah as his successor without telling his court prophet about it. The plan worked. David immediately summoned Zadok, Nathan, and Benaiah and ordered them to anoint Solomon as king and place him upon the throne (1:32-35).

Solomon's proclamation as king sent Adonijah and his supporters fleeing in every direction (1:49). But Solomon did not move against them while his father was still alive. After David's death, however, Solomon was swift and ruthless in consolidating his rule. Adonijah and Joab were killed, and Abiathar was removed from his duties as a priest. In his final words to Solomon, David commanded him, "Guard what is owed to the LORD your God, walking in his ways and observing his laws... as it is written in the Instruction from Moses" in order to assure his dynasty would continue in Israel (2:3-4). But apparently neither Solomon nor David (who advised Solomon to give both Joab and Shimei, who had been disloyal to David during Absalom's revolt, "a violent death"; 2:5-9) had any reservations about violating Moses' instruction regarding murder if it served immediate political needs.

Perhaps we can say that the first false god to lure Solomon was "royal power" (2:46b).

Solomon's Wisdom—and Foolishness (1 Kings 3–4)

The next major block in Solomon's story is devoted to his great wisdom. But things don't get off to a very promising start. Solomon looks to expand his political power through a marriage alliance with Pharaoh. Given Israel's history with Egypt, is that really such a wise idea? Additionally, he begins to carve out "exceptions" to David's admonition to "walk in [God's] laws" in that he "also sacrificed and burned incense at the shrines" (3:3), some of them certainly devoted to gods and goddesses other than the God whose ways were set out in the "Instruction from Moses."

At "the great shrine at Gibeon" (which was devoted to "the LORD"), God came to Solomon in a dream and offered to give him whatever he wished. In what is likely the clearest example of his innate wisdom, Solomon answered, "Please give your servant a discerning mind in order to govern your people and to distinguish good from evil" (3:9). That response "pleased the LORD," and so God gave Solomon not only "a wise and understanding mind," but also the "wealth and fame" that he might have asked for but had not. The only part of God's promise that was conditional was for "a very long life"; that was dependent on whether Solomon would "walk in my ways and obey my laws and commands" (3:10-14).

Across the Testaments

Jesus, Solomon, and Priorities

It was Solomon's overall reputation and association with Israel's "Golden Age" more than any particular story that lies behind Jesus' declaration that "Solomon in all of his splendor wasn't dressed like" the "lilies in the field . . . [that] don't wear themselves out with work, and they don't spin cloth" (Matthew 6:28-30). This comparison is one of a series that Jesus strings together to make the point that we should "desire first and foremost God's kingdom and God's righteousness, and all these things will be given to [us] as well" (6:33).

Solomon utilized his wisdom in a broad variety of ways, from resolving disputes between his subjects (3:16-28), to arranging the administration of his government (4:1-20), to instruction in practical philosophy and the natural sciences (4:29-34). Yet Scripture makes all these accomplishments conditional by the fact that Solomon's abilities result from God's gift to him. In a sense, then, his wisdom was a direct consequence of his faithful relationship with God.

Solomon Builds the Temple (1 Kings 5–9)

The greatest use of Solomon's wisdom was in coordinating the effort to construct the Temple in Jerusalem. Five of the eleven chapters in First

Kings devoted to Solomon's reign relate directly to the construction, furnishing, and dedication of the Temple. But as with the recounting of how Solomon received that wisdom, there is a little detail tucked away near the beginning that foreshadows trouble in the future.

In the midst of his negotiations with King Hiram of Tyre to secure the materials necessary for his projects in Jerusalem, we read, "Solomon called up a work gang of thirty thousand workers from all over Israel" (5:13). This "work gang" was not a group of volunteers, or even a cohort of unemployed tradespeople eager and grateful for the contract. They were, for all intents and purposes, slaves who had been pressed into service. Solomon may have found not only a wife in Egypt; he may also have found a method for securing the human resources necessary for his state building projects. But is it really such a wise idea to build a temple for the God who delivered a people from slavery in Egypt through the slave labor of their descendants?

About the Scripture

Corvée Labor

The technical term for these "work gangs" is corvée labor. There are indications that David also utilized this practice for some of his building projects (2 Samuel 20:24), and the use of the census process not only for taxation purposes but also to determine who could be conscripted into labor as well as the military may be a reason for God's anger at David's census (2 Samuel 24:10). Bringing an end to the practice will later be a key demand that Jeroboam sets before Rehoboam as a condition for accepting his rule (1 Kings 12:1-4). Rehoboam's promise to increase the workload demands did, in fact, limit his rule to only Judah (12:15-17).

Indeed, after the account of the Temple's dedication, the narrator closes the section by returning to "the story of the labor gang that King Solomon put together to build the LORD's temple and his own palace, as well as the stepped structure, the wall of Jerusalem, Hazor, Megiddo, and Gezer" (9:15-22). A careful distinction is drawn between non-Israelites who remained within its borders from before the period when Joshua had led the people into the land and those who were members of the Israelite tribes themselves. Only those who were descended from the previous inhabitants were pressed into service on the building projects; the Israelites were instead conscripted into military and other forms of service to the royal court. Perhaps the division was as carefully maintained as outlined here, although the reaction of Jeroboam (who was in fact "appointed... over all the work gang of Joseph's house" [the two large tribes of Ephraim and Manasseh], 11:28) and the leaders of other tribes hints that that was not the case. Yet even this restricted use of Israelites in conscripted service precisely fulfilled the warnings that Samuel had given about royal abuses of power before acceding to Israel's demand for a king "like all the other nations" (1 Samuel 8:10-20).

It took seven years to complete the construction of the Temple, and thirteen years for the construction of Solomon's palace (1 Kings 6:38–7:1).

The arrangements for the dedication of the Temple were elaborate (8:1-12). Solomon offered a lengthy prayer that the Temple would become the focal point of Israel's religious life. It was to the Temple the people were to look when there were disputes between them; during times of drought, famine, or war; and when they needed forgiveness for their sins against God. Yet Solomon himself acknowledged, "But how could God possibly live on earth? If heaven, even the highest heaven, can't contain you, how can this temple that I've built contain you?" (8:27).

Across the Testaments

A Temple Is Not Enough

In his prayer dedicating the Temple, Solomon said, "But how could God possibly live on earth? If heaven, even the highest heaven, can't contain you, how can this temple that I've built contain you?" The same observation that "the Most High doesn't live in houses built by human hands" is the climactic point in Stephen's account of Israel's history (Acts 7:47-53). Having the Temple was not enough to secure the people's faithfulness to their covenant with God: "You received the Law given by angels, but you haven't kept it."

Perhaps after all the years of preparation during his father's reign for building the Temple and all the decades of construction during his own reign, what Solomon realized was this: No matter how magnificent the structure, no matter how intricate the ceremony, no matter how involved the organization of the priests who carried it out, what ultimately mattered was the encounter with God and the relationship formed by the people with God and with each other. Despite all the work and expense, the Temple could never be more than a means to the proper end of living in relationship with God.

After the dedication ceremonies were finished, God once again came to Solomon in a dream (9:1-9). God told him, "I have set apart this temple that you built, to put my name there forever." God was likewise prepared to "establish [Solomon's] royal throne forever." But there were conditions to these promises: If either Solomon or his descendants were to "turn away" from following God and were to instead "serve other gods, and worship them," then God would "reject the temple" and bring "all this disaster on them."

Solomon's Relationship With God (1 Kings 10–11)

The completion of the Temple and the other building projects further compounded both Solomon's reputation for wisdom (see the story of the visit by the queen of Sheba, 10:1-13) and his wealth (10:14-29). What's left unstated in this report of the amassing of royal fame and fortune is what must have been their costs upon the people of Israel. We know how such extravagance is achieved by the powerful of other societies throughout human history, and there is no reason to believe things could have been any different in Solomon's Israel.

As we have seen, the narrator has been satisfied to drop only hints of these problems. The prime focus of attention in the problem with Solomon is located elsewhere. He had entered into marriages of political alliance not only with Egypt but also with many other nations "including Moabites, Ammonites, Edomites, Sidonians, and Hittites." Moreover, we are told that these were not just marriages of political expedience; "Solomon clung to these women in love," and over the years they "turned his heart after other gods" (11:1-4). Having built a temple for the Lord in Jerusalem, he then built "a shrine to Chemosh, the detestable god of Moab, and to Molech the detestable god of the Ammonites, . . . [and] the same for all his foreign wives" (11:7-8).

So God appeared to Solomon one final time. Because he had not been faithful in his relationship with God, his heirs would be limited to ruling over only his ancestral tribe of Judah. The other tribes God would hand over to another (11:11-13). And although this division of Israel would not happen during Solomon's lifetime, God began immediately to initiate the process. God sent the prophet Ahijah from Shiloh (the very place in the heart of Ephraim where Samuel had been raised by Eli in the house of God) to tell Jeroboam that he was the one into whose hands God was going to deliver the other tribes (11:29-39).

There are no signs within Solomon's story that he ever came to reject his relationship with God. Every indication is that his desire to rule the people wisely in accord with God's will was sincere. He appears to have meant every word of his dedicatory prayer for the Temple with its call for the people to turn toward "the LORD" in every time of difficulty in their lives. But all his wisdom was not enough to prevent him from being enticed by other gods. It may be that he built shrines to Astarte, Chemosh, and Milcom, but they were merely the symbols of the power, prestige, and wealth that had divided his loyalties. To acquire those things, he had made compromises, at best, in his relationship with God and the people he ruled. For the sake of power, he had come to worship the gods of other nations with whom he was in alliance. For the sake of wealth and prestige, he had once again enslaved God's people to the purposes of the king just as Pharaoh had done to the Israelites centuries earlier in Egypt. Having those things seems to have made him forget that they all had been offered as gifts from God (3:10-15); he needed no other gods to have them.

In the end, perhaps the biggest unanswered question is whether Solomon ever even made the connection. We know he believed that God indeed planned to take from his heirs all of his realm except Judah because he tried to kill Jeroboam once he learned of Ahijah's prophetic act confirming what God had told him. But this reaction was a play of raw political power, like those that had brought him to the throne to begin with. It was an act in service to other gods, not to the God to whom he had become unfaithful. As such, it was doomed to fail.

Live the Story

We may have reached a cultural point where speaking about "idols" even metaphorically is not very useful. What may be of more benefit is recognizing that even for those in the past and, yes, in the present whose religions feature physical idols, the images are in their truest essence metaphors. There is a reason mythologies contain not merely names but also descriptive appellations, such as "Pallas Athena, the goddess of war." The power and allure of the idol is never in the image itself, but in the value or thing it represents.

If our faithfulness is first to the God who is the source and the goal of all that is, we will have less difficulty in recognizing the derivative nature of all that competes with God for our loyalties. There is no point in pretending that success, fame, wealth, and similar things are nothing; they are *something*, just *not everything*. How does your attention to your *spiritual* relationship with God help you maintain proper perspective on the *things* in your life? How does that *relationship* with God provide wisdom and pattern for your *relationship* with family, friends, and community?

6.

Listening to the Prophets

1 Kings 12–22

Claim Your Story

When most people in our culture hear the words *prophet* and *prophecy*, the images that come to mind are often of mysterious or eccentric people in the past who predicted things that would happen in the distant future—still in our future, or perhaps in our present. In recent years, there has been a lot of popular buzz about Nostradamus and ancient Mayan day-counters who are claimed to have predicted that the world as we know it would end in what we call the year 2012. There is often a significant degree of pessimism and indeed fatalism associated with this view of prophecy. The predictions of the prophets have a doomsday quality, and, so the thinking goes, because the future is already set, there is little if anything we can do to change it.

Though certainly less dark and pessimistic, the ways many Christians conceive of Israel's prophets is not that different. When we think of the biblical prophets as predicting details about the coming Messiah's life centuries before Jesus' birth, we may have the same sense that what we do in our own lives can't shape the future in significant ways. But does that picture of prophecy really square with what prophets were actually doing in Israel and Judah?

How have the biblical prophecies affected your outlook?

Enter the Bible Story

The conception of prophets in Israel was quite different from the typical view in our society. To the degree that prophets cared about the future, it tended to be the immediate future, certainly within the likely lifespans of some who heard their messages. Far from a fatalistic view of the future, their goal was to change it by changing what the people were doing. The ideal prophet would be someone like Jonah, who delivered God's message that caused the people to change their ways and so avoid the dire consequences that would otherwise have come upon them (although Jonah was none too happy about it [Jonah 4], but that's a story for another time). To gain a clearer understanding of what the prophets of Israel and Judah were really all about, we will look in this chapter at some prophets whose stories are told in 1 Kings 12–22. Some will appear almost anonymously, designated simply as "a man of God" rather than by a personal name. One, Elijah, is a figure of such prominence that he is better known than some of the kings during whose reigns he carried out his ministry. And the final example, Micaiah, will present us with a troubling story regarding how difficult it could be to determine who were the true prophets in Israel and Judah (and who may be true prophets in our own day as well).

About the Scripture

Former and Latter Prophets

Christian conceptions of the canon (the list and arrangement of books in the Bible) may be subtly influencing our understanding of prophecy. In Christian Bibles, the books of Samuel, Kings, and Chronicles are part of a collection called "the Historical Books" (it also includes Joshua, Judges, Ruth, Ezra, Nehemiah, and Esther). The "Prophetic Books" begin with Isaiah and conclude with Malachi. Although, as we have seen, lots of prophets appear as characters in the stories found in "the Historical Books," we may suspect they must have had different purposes than the "writing prophets."

Within the Hebrew Bible, however, the canonical arrangement is different. The books of Samuel and Kings (but not Chronicles) are grouped within a collection called "the Prophets." (Chronicles is found in the third and final collection, called "the Writings"; the first collection is called "the Torah," otherwise known as "the books of Moses.") There is only a minor distinction made between them and the collections of prophetic oracles. Joshua, Judges, Samuel, and Kings as a sub-group are known as "the Former Prophets," while Isaiah, Jeremiah, Ezekiel, and the Twelve (Hosea though Malachi) are called "the Latter Prophets." Since stories about some of the "Latter Prophets" appear in the books called "the Former Prophets," the labels may indicate more about when the books themselves were compiled than the chronology of events within them. Be that as it may, this grouping of Samuel, Nathan, Elijah, and Elisha together with Isaiah, Jeremiah, Ezekiel, Jonah, and the rest certainly doesn't suggest that their roles as prophets were different.

Prophets in the Midst of Israel and Judah's Division (1 Kings 12–13)

Let's begin by considering the very different reactions to the first prophetic messages received by the first respective kings of Judah and Israel.

In the last chapter, we saw how courses of action already begun during Solomon's rule led to the division of the kingdom following his death. When his son Rehoboam refused to accede to the demand of Jeroboam to lessen the demands of the "work gangs" drawn from the tribes of Israel, all the tribes except Judah withdrew and made Jeroboam their king (1 Kings 12:16-21). Rehoboam returned to Jerusalem and began to amass his forces "to fight against the house of Israel and restore the kingdom" to himself. As the preparations for war were being made, "God's word came to Shemaiah the man of God." The message he was to take to Rehoboam was that the division of the kingdom was God's plan for that time, and so they were not to go to war against their Israelite relatives. "When they heard the LORD's words, they went back home, just as the LORD had said" (12:22-24). Judah's separate history began, then, by the people listening to God's message, changing their course of action, and accepting God's plan as their own.

The history of Israel apart from Judah began with Jeroboam constructing two centers of worship—one at Bethel in the south of his territory, and one at Dan far to the north—so that the people of Israel would not have to travel to Jerusalem to offer sacrifices with the possibility that their allegiance might shift back to Rehoboam (12:27-29). At each of the shrines, Jeroboam placed a golden calf. It's possible from what we know about the iconography of temples from this period that Jeroboam intended these calves to be seen as carrying God's throne upon their backs. If so, then their presence in Bethel and Dan would symbolize that God was enthroned over all of Israel and not confined to the Temple in Jerusalem. But the choice of golden calves and Jeroboam's declaration, "Look, Israel! Here are your gods who brought you out from the land of Egypt" (12:28), created a very different impression.

At the very time Jeroboam was consecrating one of these shrines, "a man of God came from Judah by God's command to Bethel" (13:1). The message the man of God brought did contain a prediction that, in the future, a king of Judah named Josiah would destroy the shrine, but he also offered a sign to prove to them that an event they would not live to see would happen: "The altar will be broken apart, and its ashes will spill out" (13:3). It's possible that this sign was in fact an invitation to avert the need for Josiah's future action. If the altar split *and* the people were to abandon it in a state of disrepair, then there would be nothing for Josiah to destroy. On the other hand, if the people did repair the split altar and resume their sacrifices at the site, Josiah would once again destroy and profane the altar by spilling its ashes.

Jeroboam ordered his guards to seize the man of God, and at that very moment, the altar split. And even though Jeroboam then pleaded with the man of God to intercede with "the LORD" on his behalf—which the prophet did—Jeroboam still "didn't change his evil ways. Instead, he continued to appoint all sorts of people as priests of the shrines" (13:33). Jeroboam and the people of Israel did not take advantage of the opportunity provided by the message from the man of God to recommit themselves to faithful relationship with God. "In this way the house of Jeroboam acted sinfully, leading to its downfall and elimination from the earth" (13:34).

Two Stories About Elijah (1 Kings 18:17–19:18; 21:1-29)

Surely one of the most beloved stories about Elijah is his contest with the prophets of Baal on Mount Carmel. Elijah positioned the contest as a way of clearly demonstrating who deserved the people's faithfulness—the God of Israel who had brought their ancestors out of Egypt, or Baal of the Canaanites in whose land they had come to live. The story is told with several touches of humor, deliberately mocking the prophets of Baal and those who would follow them (18:27). Elijah goes out of his way to make the test harder for God. He waits until it is "time for the evening offering" (18:29) before calling the people away from Baal's altar. As the temperature dropped and the sun began to set, he ordered that God's altar be flooded with water. Even with all this, when "the LORD's fire fell[,] it consumed the sacrifice, the wood, the stones, and the dust. It even licked up the water in the trench!" (18:38). Yet though the people seize Baal's prophets at Elijah's command, there is no indication in what follows that either Israel's king Ahab or the people turn completely back to God.

Baal, the God of Storm

One aspect of Elijah's confrontation with the prophets of Baal may go unnoticed by those unfamiliar with Baal's role in Canaanite mythology. Among his various associations, Baal was the god of the storm and so was often portrayed with a lightning bolt in his hand, which may be what set the terms for the contest as sending fire down to burn the sacrifices. But because Baal sent the storms, people would pray and offer sacrifices to him during times of drought. In a way, then, Elijah's contest with Baal's prophets began three years earlier when Elijah had announced to Ahab, "there will be neither dew nor rain unless I say so" (17:1; 18:1). The rain (18:41) was as essential to Elijah's victory over Baal as was the fire that consumed the sacrifice.

Indeed, Elijah's own actions would suggest quite the opposite. He "was terrified" by Queen Jezebel's threat to kill him (19:3) and eventually took refuge in a cave on Mount Horeb in the Sinai peninsula, where all of Judah would have been a buffer between him and Ahab. There he claimed, "I'm the only one left" of all those who had been faithful to God (19:14). But God assured him that he was not alone: "I have preserved those who remain in Israel, totaling seven thousand—all those whose knees haven't bowed down to Baal and whose mouths haven't kissed him" (19:18).

Later, Elijah was even successful in reaching Ahab. God sent Elijah to Ahab for the last time after Jezebel had conspired to obtain Naboth's vineyard for him (21:1-16). God's message for Ahab was both harsh and vivid in its details: "In the same place where dogs licked up Naboth's blood, they will lick up your own blood" (21:19). Notwithstanding the narrator's commentary that "truly there has never been anyone like Ahab who sold out by doing evil in the LORD's eyes" (21:25), when Ahab heard Elijah's words, he began to fast and perform the rituals of mourning as signs of his repentance. When Ahab humbled himself before God, it altered the course of his future, if not also that of his household (21:27-29).

Across the Testaments

Elijah and Jesus

The association of Elijah with Mounts Carmel and Horeb calls to mind his role in the story about Jesus' transformation on a mountain (Luke 9:28-36). Elijah appeared with Moses and discussed with Jesus the "departure [Greek, *exodus*], which [Jesus] would achieve in Jerusalem" (9:31). Together, Moses and Elijah personified the Torah and the Prophets, the Scriptures that guided Jesus as he carried out God's plan for redemption. Scripture remains our primary guide for knowing how to live faithfully according to God's plan.

Jehoshaphat and Ahab Consult With Micaiah (1 Kings 22:1-38)

The final story about prophets in First Kings is a troubling one. Ahab (referred to throughout this story simply as, "Israel's king") wanted to enlist the aid of Judah's king, Jehoshaphat, in regaining control of Ramoth-gilead from Aram. Jehoshaphat was willing to join in the campaign, "But . . . first let's see what the LORD has to say" (22:5). They gathered some four hundred prophets (none of them prophets of Baal or other Canaanite gods), who were unanimous in their view: " 'Attack!' the prophets answered. 'The LORD will hand it over to the king' " (22:6b). One of them, Zedekiah, would eventually go so far as to place iron horns on his head and announce, "This is what the LORD says: With these horns you will gore the Arameans until there's nothing left of them!" (22:11).

Somehow, Jehoshaphat still was not convinced: "Isn't there any other prophet of the LORD whom we could ask?" So Ahab told him about another prophet, Micaiah, "but I hate him because he never prophesies anything good about me, only bad" (22:7-8). Once Micaiah arrived, his word is in agreement with the others: "Attack and win!" (22:15). So certain is Ahab from his past experience that this cannot be the message from Micaiah that he says, "How many times must I demand that you tell me the truth when you speak in the name of the LORD?" (22:16).

It is at this point that what has been almost comical turns troubling (22:19-28). Micaiah now announces that his vision was of "all Israel scattered on the hills like sheep without a shepherd!" He proceeds to recount a vision of "the LORD enthroned with all the heavenly forces" seeking council on how to send Ahab to his death in battle at Ramoth-gilead. The proposal that won God's approval came from one particular spirit that said, "I will be a lying spirit in the mouth of all his prophets." The other prophets didn't take kindly to this suggestion. Zedekiah struck him and asked, "Just how did the LORD's spirit leave me to speak to you?" Micaiah's response was that the course of events would demonstrate who is right.

Ahab doesn't accept Micaiah's message enough to cancel the campaign, but he does put enough faith in it to disguise himself in battle so as not to draw attention to himself as the king of Israel. The ploy didn't work: "someone randomly shot an arrow that struck Israel's king between the joints in his armor" (22:34), and Ahab bled to death from the wound.

What are we to make of this strange story? Is God in the habit of sending "a lying spirit" in order to lead people to their ruin? (And don't try to brush this off as some kind of "Old Testament thing" that needn't worry us now, because a strikingly similar view is found in 2 Thessalonians 2:11.) Thankfully, such stories are so rare in Scripture that we can rule out the possibility that God regularly sends messengers to deceive people. And notice that even here, Ahab recognized the inconsistency in Micaiah's original message. Had he followed through on what he knew to be true and was confirmed by Micaiah's second message (as opposed to what he wanted to be true), then he could have avoided dying in the battle for Ramoth-gilead.

Probably the more important lesson we need to take from this story is that there are a lot of people who believe themselves in all sincerity to be messengers from God. Some of them, like Micaiah, have genuine insight and wisdom to share. Others like Zedekiah may think they do, but they don't. As unlikely as it may seem, Ahab is probably our guide in such situations, at least regarding how to recognize a true prophet. Who is speaking the things that are consistent with God's messages in the past, foremost among them those that are in Scripture? Whose *message* is consistent with the person of the *messenger* as one who faithfully lives in accord with God's plan? There are many prophets still out there, but if we measure their messages with what we know to be a faithful manner of life then we, like

Jehoshaphat, will know when it is time to ask, "Isn't there any other prophet of the LORD whom we could ask?"

Live the Story

The primary concern of Israel and Judah's prophets was with the lives of their contemporaries, not with those who would live in a future they would never see. Some scholars have tried to capture this difference of emphasis by saying that the biblical prophets engaged less in "foretelling" the future than in "forth-telling" the truth about their societies and the abuses of the powerful against those they pushed to the margins. In some ways, it would be easier if God's messengers only told us what a future beyond our control will be like. That would absolve us of any responsibility to try to shape that future for the better. But instead, God's true prophets confront us with truths we would rather not hear and challenge us to change our behavior and so change the course both of our lives and of those who will follow us.

Whom do you see as God's prophets in the world today? Who have been God's messengers to you personally, reminding you of God's ways and encouraging you to live in accord with them? What prophetic message may God be asking you to deliver to others, both by what you say and by what you do?

7.

Everyone's an Example, Whether Good or Bad

2 Kings 1–25

Claim Your Story

Pick just about any area of modern life, and you will be able to find a "top ten" list describing it published somewhere. But even within a single area, you will find competing ways for assessing what makes something the best. Take movies, for example. Do you determine the best movies of the year based on their box office receipts or based upon awards they receive? And if you decide to use awards as your criterion, do you go with awards given by people within the industry (say, the Academy Awards), by film writers and critics (the Golden Globes), or by movie fans (the People's Choice Awards)?

Suppose you need to have information about what is best in some area of life far more consequential than movies. What is the best treatment course for a particular disease or ailment? What is the best financial plan to provide for yourself when you can no longer work, or for your family should you die unexpectedly? Who provides the best model for how to live faithfully in communion with God? Whose example should be avoided? Who gets to decide what is best, and on what basis do they make the decision?

What personal life events have caused you to have to consider questions such as these?

Enter the Bible Story

For the author of First and Second Kings, the criterion for determining who were the best (and who were the worst) rulers was very straightforward. If the king followed the example of David in faithfulness to the God of Israel, then that king went onto the "best" list. If the king followed the example of Jeroboam in worshiping other gods and encouraging the people to do the same, then that king went onto the "worst" list. There may have been a few—only a very few (Solomon comes to mind)—who would seem to fall somewhere in the middle, but even they ultimately went on the "worst" list if they had anything short of undivided loyalty to God (see 1 Kings 11:6-13). By this standard, every king of the Northern Kingdom of Israel from Jeroboam to Hoshea was on the author's "worst" list.

For this study of Second Kings, we will focus on a few leaders who made the "best" list. In order to include a representative from Israel, we will have to draw in one of the great prophets, Elisha (for reasons we have just seen in Chapter 6). From Judah, we will consider two kings who were among the very "best" in terms of the writer's criterion; however, looking at their lives more broadly, we will find that they were both positive and negative examples. We will end, as Second Kings itself does, by briefly considering Jehoiachin, the last king of Judah, who even in failure becomes a symbol of hope.

About the Scripture

Interpreting History Theologically

The literary structuring of First and Second Kings from the point when the kingdom is divided emerges from summary statements about each king of Israel and Judah. These include information about when his reign began and ended, important events during his reign, and a theological assessment of the king. Because the sequence alternates irregularly between Israel and Judah depending upon the length of a king's reign (see for example, 1 Kings 14:19–16:34), this pattern can make the relative chronology of events difficult to follow. But these biblical books are concerned with providing a theological interpretation of events in Israel and Judah and not simply providing data for constructing a timeline.

Elisha (2 Kings 2:1–13:20)

We first meet Elisha in 1 Kings 19:16-21, where he accepts a call to be Elijah's disciple, but he doesn't come into his prophetic work until Second Kings. As the understudy to Elijah, Elisha definitely had a tough act to follow. Such was the role into which Elisha was cast, yet he succeeded by remaking the part as his own. Whereas Elijah's story places him primarily playing opposite Ahab in an effort to turn the king and so the people back to a faithful relationship with God, more attention is given in Elisha's story to his interactions with the people rather than royalty. He engages people from all aspects of the society, whether poor (4:1-7) or rich (4:8-37). He even engaged those who were Israel's enemies, always to make the point that Israel's God was the only God.

It was because of Elisha's reputation as one who mediated God's miraculous power to people that he even came to the attention of Naaman, a general for the king of Aram (5:1-27). During an Aramean raid on Israel, a young girl had been taken captive and had become a slave to Naaman's wife. It was her confidence that Elisha would be able to bring about a cure for Naaman's debilitating skin disease that led him to ask permission from the king of Aram to seek Elisha's help. Naaman presented a letter from his king to the king of Israel (though unnamed in the story, the sequence of episodes in the Elisha narrative suggests it was probably Joram), who believed the request to cure the military commander of his disease was simply a pretext for renewed hostilities. Elisha himself was undaunted by the request: "Let the man come to me. Then he'll know that there's a prophet in Israel" (5:8). And when Naaman's skin was restored after he followed Elisha's instruction to wash himself seven times in the muddy waters of the slowly meandering Jordan River, he confessed more than just that Elisha was a prophet: "Now I know for certain that there's no God anywhere on earth except in Israel" (5:15).

Elisha was not unconcerned with Israel's monarchy, however, and he played a key role in completing Elijah's work in that regard. We noted in the previous chapter that while Ahab's repentance late in life forestalled

Across the Testaments

God's Presence and Miraculous Signs

It is not just modern skeptics who raise the question about why some people have miraculous recoveries while others suffer and die. Jesus himself faced the same challenge early in his ministry from his neighbors in Nazareth (Luke 4:23-27) and included Naaman among his examples: "There were also many persons with skin diseases in Israel during the time of the prophet Elisha, but none of them were cleansed. Instead, Naaman the Syrian was cleansed."

You don't have to read all that closely to see that while Jesus acknowledges the fact that God does not heal everyone, he doesn't offer any explanation as to why that is the case. Rather, Jesus simply uses the presence of Elijah, Elisha, and himself working among those who were not healed to demonstrate that the absence of the miraculous does not equate with the absence of God. Even in difficult situations, we can discern God's presence if we look for it rather than just for a miraculous sign.

God's judgment on him personally, it didn't remove the threat of judgment from his family (1 Kings 21:27-29). It was Elisha who sent a messenger to anoint Jehu as king of Israel and direct him to "strike down...Ahab's family" (2 Kings 9:1-10). Jehu was commended for his role as an instrument of God's judgment on Ahab's family, but still was criticized because he "wasn't careful to keep the LORD God of Israel's Instruction with all his heart" and "didn't deviate from the sins that Jeroboam had caused Israel to commit" (10:30-31). If Elisha had hoped he had found in Jehu a leader for Israel who could restore the people to the path of walking faithfully with God, then he must have been disappointed.

Hezekiah (2 Kings 18–20)

Any mystery about how Judah's king Hezekiah would rate on the writer's scale is removed right at the outset. Not only are we told that he "did what was right in the LORD's eyes, just as his ancestor David had done," but he also "removed the shrines...smashed the sacred pillars and cut down the sacred pole," even going so far as to destroy a relic associated with Moses because it had become an object of veneration, namely "the bronze snake" Moses had raised on a pole (18:3-4; see Numbers 21:4-9).

But Hezekiah's faithfulness to God didn't mean he never waivered in his trust that God would be with him. He had seen the Northern Kingdom of Israel fall to the Assyrian king Shalmaneser (18:9-12), and Judah was the next stop once the current Assyrian ruler Sennacherib resumed the military campaign. When Jerusalem itself came under siege, Hezekiah "ripped his clothes, covered himself with mourning clothes, and went to the LORD's temple" in order to "send up a prayer for those few people who still survive" (19:1-4). It fell to the prophet Isaiah to repeatedly reassure Hezekiah that God would indeed preserve Jerusalem even though the siege would be long and difficult (19:5-7, 20-34). The siege was broken when "the LORD's messenger" went through the Assyrian camp one night and "struck down one hundred eighty-five thousand soldiers" (19:35-36; compare 2 Samuel 24:15-17).

Shortly after the Assyrians had withdrawn, Hezekiah became seriously ill. In response to his prayers, God told him through Isaiah that fifteen years would be added to his life (20:1-6). That extension of his life proved to be a mixed blessing for Judah. During his recovery, Hezekiah received Merodach-baladan, the son of Babylon's king, as an emissary and showed him all of the royal and Temple treasures (20:12-13). Although Babylon was itself under the shadow of Assyria at that time, Isaiah announced to Hezekiah "the LORD's word" that in time, the Babylonians would take Judah's wealth, and some of Hezekiah's descendants would be taken into exile in the palace of the Babylonian king. Nevertheless, Hezekiah was pleased by this oracle "because he thought: There will be peace and security in my lifetime" (20:19).

That Hezekiah could be considered without equal "among all of Judah's kings," both before and after him, even in light of these stories about him should be understood less as an indictment against those kings than as a kind of encouragement to us all. Being faithful to God is much more a factor of living in relationship with God than it is a blind confidence that God will always protect us from all harm. It is the commitment to doing what is "right in the LORD's eyes" more than perfectly meeting that commitment. It admits the possibility of doubt, even if it also denies the possibility of looking to anything else to assume God's rightful place in our lives.

Josiah (2 Kings 22:1–23:30)

Although four of his descendants would follow him as kings of Judah, Josiah was the last one the writer would commend because he "walked in the ways of his ancestor David—not deviating from it even a bit to the right or left" (22:2). Early in his reign, he ordered that Temple treasury funds be used to pay for repairs that were needed at the Temple. During those renovations, the high priest Hilkiah found the "Instruction scroll" in the Temple (22:8).

From the reported reactions of those who read the scroll, two things seem to have stood out within its contents. First, the scroll warned that God would "bring disaster" upon the people if they were to "desert [the LORD]" and begin to worship other gods (22:16-17). Second, it provided specific directives for the celebration of the Passover. There is some uncertainty from the phrasing in 23:21-23 as to whether the people had centuries earlier stopped observing the Passover altogether or that their Passover practices were different from those prescribed in the scroll. (The latter would seem to be implied by the notice in 2 Chronicles 30 about a particular Passover observance during Hezekiah's reign.)

There was good news related to the discovery of the scroll as well. The prophetess Huldah indicated that God was pleased by Josiah's response to it: "Because your heart was broken and you submitted before the LORD when you heard what I said about this place and its citizens . . . I have listened to you, declares the LORD. . . . You won't experience the disaster I am about to bring on this place" (22:19-20). Notice how this result fits in with both the cyclical pattern of the Deuteronomistic History and the function of prophets. As so many times before, the people have turned away from God and are facing judgment. By returning to God, however, they have foreclosed the impending judgment—at least until the cycle repeats itself once again.

Perhaps it was out of a hope that the cycle could be broken once and for all that Josiah so zealously worked to remove every vestige of shrines to other gods, not only from Judah (23:1-14) but also from what had been the territory of the Northern Kingdom of Israel. (Note especially the excursion to Bethel in 23:15-18, and the mention of "all the shrines on the

About the Scripture

The Instruction Scroll

Based on the inferences in 2 Kings 22–23 about the contents of the "Instruction Scroll," together with Josiah's emphasis on removing all shrines other than the Temple in Jerusalem (23:8-20), there is general agreement among scholars that the scroll is somehow related to Deuteronomy. There is considerable debate among scholars, however, about whether the scroll was a copy of Deuteronomy in the form we know or an earlier form, and whether it was a catalyst for Josiah's reforms or a response to them.

high hills... throughout the cities of Samaria" in 23:19.) But if that was Josiah's intention, it was a hope that would not be realized. The die, as it were, had already been cast: "the LORD didn't turn away from the great rage that burned against Judah on account of all that [King] Manasseh [Hezekiah's idol-worshiping son] had done" (23:26).

So, if Josiah was such a positive example in his religious reforms, in what way was he also a negative one? Suffice it to say that he was not as strong a military leader as he was a religious one. For reasons that are not explained, Josiah interjected himself into a war between the Egyptians and the Assyrians. He positioned his troops to halt the northern advance of Pharaoh Neco's army up the Mediterranean coast where they would emerge from a pass through the Carmel Ridge onto the plain at Megiddo. Josiah was killed in the battle, and Judah remained under Egyptian domination until the arrival of the Babylonians. Although he had consulted with the prophetess Huldah about what he should do in response to the discovery of the "Instruction scroll," there is no indication that Josiah sought God's leading in any way before this military endeavor. Perhaps if he had, the end of his life might have been different. It is not enough for us to seek God's presence with and direction for us with regard to religious or spiritual things. We need to be open to God's leading in every aspect of our lives.

Jehoiachin (2 Kings 24:8–25:30)

Little is said about what Jehoiachin actually did beyond the notice that "he did what was evil in the LORD's eyes, just as all his ancestors had done" (that is, he worshiped gods other than the God of Israel) and that he surrendered Jerusalem to the Babylonians and was taken into exile (24:9-12). At least by that course of action he temporarily staved off the total destruction of the city. But it was only temporary. His uncle—installed as king by the Babylonians who also gave him the name Zedekiah—rebelled against the Babylonians about a decade later. When they took Jerusalem that time, they burned the city to the ground and tore down its walls. "So Judah was exiled from its land" (25:21b).

Yet when Second Kings draws to its close (25:27-30), we see that after thirty-seven years of exile, Jehoiachin has been released from prison by Babylon's new king, Awil-merodach. If an heir of David still survives, then perhaps there is at least a sliver of hope. If the king and the people will learn the lesson of their history and the "Instruction scroll," if they will commit themselves solely to the God of Israel, then maybe—just maybe—the cycle can come around one more time. And this time maybe they will be able to stop it at the stage where God has yet again delivered them from their enemies. But that even after thirty-seven years of imprisonment Jehoiachin is able so easily to insinuate himself at the king of Babylon's table, with all that implies (see Daniel 1:8-16), would suggest that it was a sliver of hope at best.

Live the Story

My paternal grandfather was fond of saying, "Everyone serves a purpose in life, even if it is just to be a bad example." He usually thought it was fairly obvious who the bad examples were. Perhaps the writer of Second Kings would have agreed. Certainly that author had a simple test for assessing the rulers of Israel and Judah. Continue in "the sins that Jeroboam had caused Israel to commit" (10:31)—Bad. Do "just as his ancestor David had done" (18:3)—Good. Thankfully, the stories told about at least some of the kings that go beyond what is contained in summary notices about their rule give us a good bit more to go on than just that.

Each of the figures focused on in this study lived in times of particular uncertainty. Elisha during a coup in Israel. Hezekiah ruling Judah as

Israel came to its end. Josiah when Judah was caught in between the aspirations of much larger empires. Jehoiachin as Jerusalem fell to Babylon.

What examples of faithfulness do you find in their lives? What weaknesses would you work to avoid? How do their lives help you identify God's presence in yours, especially as you move through uncertain times?

8.

Re-forming Community in the Context of Exile

First and Second Chronicles

Claim Your Story

Two themes can be found in much of the current reflection about the American church: "exile" and "emergent." For some outside the church, the use of these terms as descriptions for the church might appear both a bit strained and inconsistent. It is obviously not the case that Christians have been banished/exiled from the country. Moreover, since "exiled" would mean that you'd have been in the place before (otherwise how can you have been forced out?), in what sense could one say that the church is also "emerging," making its way into the culture for the *first* time?

Yet for many Christians these words resonate deeply in their experience of the church. While the church is certainly still present within our society, it has just as surely been "exiled" from the place it occupied in the culture of the mid-twentieth century. There is also a strong sense the church will never again be what it was, even as there is an equally strong sense that what it will be in the future is still "emerging" and so remains unclear. But how can the emerging church really be the church if it doesn't maintain some continuity with what it has always been?

Enter the Bible Story

For the first readers of Chronicles, there was nothing metaphorical about the cultural exile they had experienced. True, very few inhabitants of Judah had been marched off to Babylon by the invading forces that had destroyed Jerusalem and its Temple, and those that had were almost certainly from the highest level of society. But aspects of their society that had defined key parts of everyone's identity as a people were no more. Nothing remained of the glorious Temple constructed during Solomon's rule. No descendant of David ruled as king over all of Israel. Indeed, no one remained who had living memory of either the Temple or king.

Nevertheless, some things were emerging from the rubble that could lay some claim to a connection to what had come before. A descendant of David, Zerubbabel, had served as governor of what was by then the Persian province of Judah. He had participated in the laying of the foundation for a new house for God in Jerusalem (Ezra 3:8-13). Yet by the time Chronicles was written, five generations had passed since Zerubbabel (1 Chronicles 3:17-20). It was clear that while there was some continuity with what had existed before the Exile, things were not going to return to what they had been before. The question behind Chronicles, and of concern to many of the writer's contemporaries, was how understanding the past could help them perceive God's presence as they moved into an uncertain future.

Both the nature of First and Second Chronicles themselves and the amount of material we have to cover will require this final chapter in our study to be rather different than the ones that precede it. To this point we have tried to "enter the Bible story" to learn how it may be both a lens to help us see God's presence and activity in our lives and a structure to help us tell the stories of our own spiritual journeys. But, as we shall see, the writer of Chronicles has already done both of those things. Chronicles uses selected stories from the books of Samuel and Kings (and a few others as well) as a lens for viewing Judah's postexilic landscape and borrows some of its structure as a frame upon which to construct its retelling of the story for a new audience in that new day. So, rather than once more enter the stories of David, Solomon, and all the rest within Chronicles' narrative, in this study we will enter the story of Chronicles itself. To put it differently, we will try to watch what the writer *is doing* rather than what the writer *has done*.

Relationship Between Chronicles and Samuel/Kings

In terms of the span of history it covers, Chronicles overlaps the books of Samuel and Kings. First Chronicles begins with Adam, but its reports are almost exclusively genealogical prior to the events recounted concerning Saul's death at the battle on Mount Gilboa (1 Chronicles 10:1-6; 1 Samuel 31:1-6). (We will return to what the writer may have hoped to accomplish by beginning with nine chapters worth of genealogies and lists later.) Second Chronicles ends with a brief paragraph about the order by Persia's king Cyrus for Judah's exiles in Babylon to return to their homeland to rebuild the Temple (2 Chronicles 36:22-23; Ezra 1:1-4).

But Chronicles does more than just overlap the historical period covered in Samuel and Kings. As a side-by-side reading of their accounts of Saul's death just cited shows, Chronicles at points borrows from those earlier books word-for-word. Much as in the case of doing side-by-side readings of the Synoptic Gospels (Matthew, Mark, and Luke, which also share at points word-for-word similarity), a great deal can be learned by paying attention to what the writer of Chronicles chooses to borrow, decides to leave aside, and adds to the work of his predecessor.

First, the writer of Chronicles was interested in the Davidic dynasty and so almost exclusively in the history of Judah. As we have seen, none of the stories about Saul are reported except the one about his death. After the other Israelite tribes separate from Judah early in Rehoboam's rule (2 Chronicles 10), the kings of Israel are only mentioned when they come up in the stories about Judah's kings (for example, Jehoshaphat's involvement with Ahab [and Micaiah]; 2 Chronicles 18:1–19:3). Nevertheless, one of the writer's favorite expressions is "all Israel"; it appears 44 times across Chronicles, including 12 times after the division between Judah and the other tribes (primarily in stories about Hezekiah; 2 Chronicles 29–32). In a sense, the story of "all Israel" is bound up in and told through the story of Judah.

Second, the writer's interest in the Davidic dynasty is primarily with regard to its role in supporting the religious life of Israel (the people, not the nation) through the Temple in Jerusalem. While Chronicles includes nothing about David's affair with Bathsheba and the tumultuous events that followed until Solomon succeeded him (2 Samuel 11–1 Kings 2), it adds a lot of material about preparations that David made for the construction of the Temple that actually began during Solomon's reign (1 Chronicles 22–29). Likewise, there is a substantial section dealing with Hezekiah's rededication of the Temple (2 Chronicles 29:3-36) not found in Second Kings, and a much expanded report of his other religious reforms (compare 2 Chronicles 30–31 with 2 Kings 18:3-4).

About the Scripture

How *Israel* Is Used in Scripture

Throughout the Scriptures, the name *Israel* is used in several different ways:

(1) It is the new name that is given to Jacob after he wrestled with the "man" on the banks of the Jabbok, "because [he had] struggled with God and with men and won" (Genesis 32:22-32, especially verse 28). Each of the other uses derives from this one.

(2) *Israel* is used to refer to any and all of the people who belonged to one of the traditional "twelve tribes of Israel" descended from Jacob's sons. It is this usage that allows books like Chronicles and Ezekiel to call the people "Israel" long after many of the tribes had lost their particular identity following the Assyrian invasions of the northern and southern kingdoms.

(3) Sometimes, *Israel* is used in the restrictive sense of the nation formed from those tribes that refused to join Judah in recognizing Rehoboam's rule. Jeroboam was the first ruler of this "Northern Kingdom of Israel."

(4) Finally, the broadest use of the term *Israel* in Christian tradition is as a title for all the people of God regardless of race or ethnicity (Galatians 6:16).

It has sometimes been suggested that Chronicles attempts to "whitewash" the more sordid aspects of the reputation of David and his successors by this pattern of omissions and additions. But given how much of the accounts of the failure of Judah's kings to maintain the people's faithfulness to God is taken over from Kings word-for-word, that was probably not the primary motivation. More likely, what we have is an example of how Scripture has often been read and used by God's people. The writer has a particular concern, namely, how proper attention by the people to their relationship with and worship of God may help them recognize God's presence with them in their radically changed circumstances, and just as importantly, spare them from repeating mistakes of the past. The parts of the story in Samuel and Kings (and other sources; see, for example, 2 Chronicles 32:32) that provided the pattern for both what should be done and for what should be avoided are brought forward and presented in a new way for that later time. Some scholars have even compared Chronicles to midrash, a particular Jewish practice of interpreting Scripture in just this way.

Structure of Chronicles

There are four major sections in Chronicles: the genealogies (1 Chronicles 1–9), the stories of David (1 Chronicles 10–29) and Solomon (2 Chronicles 1–9), and the path to exile and beyond (2 Chronicles 10–36). Each section has its particular role to play in the overall effort to define the people and their relationship with God in their new circumstances. Let's face it: few people are going to be willing to read (and much less be excited about the prospect of doing so) through the nine chapters of genealogies and lists that begin Chronicles. If the writer had a modern literary agent, that agent's response would have to be: "What on earth are you thinking?!" But in one way, that cry of exasperation reveals the point. By beginning with Adam and working down to Israel (that is, the patriarch Jacob; 1 Chronicles 1:1–2:2), the writer establishes who the people of Israel are among the other peoples of the earth. The focus then shifts to "Judah's family" (2:3) and ultimately "David's family" (3:1), once again showing how the Davidic dynasty relates to its own tribe, and then subsequently to "all Israel" (which, we have noted, is a special interest of this writer) through genealogies of "Simeon's family" (4:24) and those of Reuben (5:1) and the rest. Special attention is also given to "Levi's family" (6:1-81) because of their particular responsibilities in the Temple. Above all, it is the history implicit in all these family lists that establishes that those who have resettled the land following the "exile in Babylon" (9:1b-3) are indeed the same people who have been in relationship with God—sometimes faithfully, sometimes not.

About the Scripture

"An Account of the Days"

Like the books of Samuel and Kings, First and Second Chronicles were originally a single book. Its Hebrew title might be translated as, "An Account of the Days." It appears at the very end of the section known as "the Writings," making it the very last book in the Jewish Scriptures. At various times it has been suggested that Chronicles was composed by the same author who wrote Ezra-Nehemiah (also a single book in Hebrew), but that view finds less support among scholars now.

The remaining three sections relate in different ways to the centrality of the Temple within the life of the people. David's story is stripped down almost to the bare essentials needed to explain why the Temple should have been located in Jerusalem, why God blocks David's desire to build the Temple, and finally the preparations he began so that the Temple could be built by his successor. Solomon's story focuses on his relationship with God and the building of the Temple, and leaves aside the material from First Kings regarding the other shrines he had constructed and the breach to his faithfulness in relationship to God that they demonstrate. The final section, from Rehoboam to Cyrus's order to rebuild the Temple, shows the consequences both of failing to remain faithful to God and of repentance and restoration of that relationship (the latter especially through the extra attention given to Hezekiah and Josiah). Now that even the other nations have recognized the importance of God's Temple (through Persia's king Cyrus; 2 Chronicles 36:22-23), the clear path into their future relationship with God is through proper worship at the place where God's presence is most profound on the earth, the Temple in Jerusalem.

Key Themes in Chronicles

Three particular themes emerge from the way the writer of Chronicles retells Israel's story. First, just as the author himself relies on the sacred history of Israel to interpret the situation facing the people after the Exile, so the prophets and kings who offer speeches in the retelling of that history often refer back to the earlier portions of the story and the words of the prophets known to them in their particular settings. To take just one example, Jehoshaphat instructed the judges he appointed to administer cities in Judah that they must "respect the LORD and act accordingly, because there can be no injustice, playing favorites, or taking bribes when it comes to the LORD our God" (2 Chronicles 19:4-8). Those instructions borrow language from Deuteronomy 10:17. One key to living in proper relationship with God in the present is to learn from the example of those who walked with God in the past.

Second, we have seen how Chronicles places great emphasis upon the Temple in Jerusalem as the place on earth where God's presence is most to be found. That is the reason for the centrality of the Temple in the worship of God and, consequently, for the centrality of Judah and Jerusalem among the people of God. However, the picture painted in Chronicles is not one that decisively excludes any people other than Judah from enjoying this relationship with God. Judah is in a sense broader than just the descendants of the patriarch Judah, as time and again Chronicles speaks to and about Judah as "all Israel." In similar fashion, Israel may be broader than just the descendants of Jacob as representative of all the people who may be in relationship with God. In his prayer dedicating the Jerusalem Temple, Solomon spoke about "the foreigner who isn't from your people Israel, but who comes from a distant country" to worship God in the Temple. He prays that God will answer the foreigner's prayers "so that all the people of the earth may know your reputation and revere you" (2 Chronicles 6:32-33).

Across the Testaments

A House of Prayer for All Nations

Despite Solomon's prayer and the later hope of the writer of Chronicles, the Temple eventually became a symbol of exclusivism rather than a place of God's reaching out to all people. Over the ensuing centuries, the Temple had at various times become a symbol of Jewish resistance against foreign occupiers. Jesus decried this practice: "Hasn't it been written, *My house will be called a house of prayer for all nations?* But you've turned it into *a hideout for crooks*" (Mark 11:17). The specific word Jesus uses for "crooks" didn't refer to just common thieves; it was also used for revolutionaries and insurrectionists. Whenever the symbols of God's concern for all the world are restricted by some as applicable only to themselves at the exclusion of others, then those people have corrupted the sacred traditions of God's people.

In the very ending of the book, that possibility becomes reality again through the foreigner Cyrus (2 Chronicles 36:22-23).

Finally, the writer of Chronicles works to introduce an element of hope into the story of God's people, because hope was one thing that was desperately needed by his contemporaries. Like 1 Kings 14:21-31, Chronicles reports how Judah was invaded by Egypt's king Shishak after it had "been unfaithful to the LORD" (2 Chronicles 12:1-12). But unlike the account in Kings, it concludes with this short note: "When Rehoboam submitted, the LORD was no longer angry with him, and total destruction was avoided. There were, after all, some good things still in Judah." Even in the story of Manasseh, Judah's most notorious king (see 2 Kings 21:1-18), Chronicles introduces new material that reports a change—albeit one achieved through harsh means (2 Chronicles 33:10-19). The Assyrians once again laid siege to Jerusalem as they had during his father Hezekiah's reign. This time they "captured Manasseh with hooks, bound him with bronze chains, and carried him off to Babylon." While in exile, Manasseh "truly submit[ted] himself to the God of his ancestors," so God "restored him to his rule in Jerusalem." Once back there, he undertook many reforms to reestablish the people in relationship with God.

In these three themes are found the heart of Chronicles' message both to the people of its own time and of ours. The pattern for how we are to live our lives in relationship with God are to be found in the Scriptures; however, it will be only a pattern because the particular circumstances we face will be different. We learn how to apply that pattern through recognizing those places where God is present and by staying in faithful relationship with God. But even if we should sometimes fail, there remains hope when we once again renew our relationship with God and submit to God's instruction. That was the message contained in the story of Judah's kings for those emerging from exile in Babylon, and it is the message contained in Chronicles for the church today as it emerges from its exile experience into the future God is preparing for it.

Live the Story

Continuity always requires connection with the past, but if it does not also reflect change, then it is not really "continuity" but rather simply "identity." Moving into the future must entail an element of leaving the past behind. For the writer of Chronicles, part of what seems to have been left behind is the expectation that an heir to David would once more be the king over God's people. The path to the future led through the Temple system that David had established as a pattern for how the people might be in relationship with God, not through political restoration. The glorious age of David and Solomon was not coming back, but that didn't mean new glories in their relationship with God were impossible.

Suppose you were given the task of retelling the history of the church in the West, say, since the time of the Protestant Reformation and the Catholic Counter-Reformation for the purpose of helping Christians understand what is happening in the church of the twenty-first century. What lessons would you draw from the ways Chronicles retells the history of Israel and Judah to its postexilic community? What patterns in its story would help you discern God's presence in the history of the church? Where would you find the signs for hope that would encourage people in their relationships with God?

Leader Guide

People often view the Bible as a maze of obscure people, places, and events from centuries ago and struggle to relate it to their daily lives. IMMERSION invites us to experience the Bible as a record of God's loving revelation to humankind. These studies recognize our emotional, spiritual, and intellectual needs and welcome us into the Bible story and into deeper faith.

As leader of an IMMERSION group, you will help participants to encounter the Word of God and the God of the Word that will lead to new creation in Christ. You do not have to be an expert to lead; in fact, you will participate with your group in listening to and applying God's life-transforming Word to your lives. You and your group will explore the building blocks of the Christian faith through key stories, people, ideas, and teachings in every book of the Bible. You will also explore the bridges and points of connection between the Old and New Testaments.

Choosing and Using the Bible

The central goal of IMMERSION is engaging the members of your group with the Bible in a way that informs their minds, forms their hearts, and transforms the way they live out their Christian faith. Participants will need this study book and a Bible. IMMERSION is an excellent accompaniment to the Common English Bible (CEB). It shares with the CEB four common aims: clarity of language, faith in the Bible's power to transform lives, the emotional expectation that people will find the love of God, and the rational expectation that people will find the knowledge of God.

Other recommended study Bibles include *The New Interpreter's Study Bible* (NRSV), *The New Oxford Annotated Study Bible* (NRSV), *The HarperCollins Study Bible* (NRSV), the *NIV and TNIV Study Bibles*, and the *Archaeological Study Bible* (NIV). Encourage participants to use more than one translation. *The Message: The Bible in Contemporary Language* is a modern paraphrase of the Bible, based on the original languages. Eugene H. Peterson has created a masterful presentation of the Scripture text, which is best used alongside rather than in place of the CEB or another primary English translation.

One of the most reliable interpreters of the Bible's meaning is the Bible itself. Invite participants first of all to allow Scripture to have its say. Pay attention to context. Ask questions of the text. Read every passage with curiosity, always seeking to answer the basic Who? What? Where? When? and Why? questions.

Bible study groups should also have handy essential reference resources in case someone wants more information or needs clarification on specific words, terms, concepts, places, or people mentioned in the Bible. A Bible dictionary, Bible atlas, concordance, and one-volume Bible commentary together make for a good, basic reference library.

The Leader's Role

An effective leader prepares ahead. This leader guide provides easy-to-follow, step-by-step suggestions for leading a group. The key task of the leader is to guide discussion and activities that will engage heart and head and will invite faith development. Discussion questions are included, and you may want to add questions posed by you or your group. Here are suggestions for helping your group engage Scripture:

State questions clearly and simply.

Ask questions that move Bible truths from "outside" (dealing with concepts, ideas, or information about a passage) to "inside" (relating to the experiences, hopes, and dreams of the participants).

Work for variety in your questions, including compare and contrast, information recall, motivation, connections, speculation, and evaluation.

Avoid questions that call for yes-or-no responses or answers that are obvious.

Don't be afraid of silence during a discussion. It often yields especially thoughtful comments.

Test questions before using them by attempting to answer them yourself.

When leading a discussion, pay attention to the mood of your group by "listening" with your eyes as well as your ears.

Guidelines for the Group

IMMERSION is designed to promote full engagement with the Bible for the purpose of growing faith and building up Christian community. While much can be gained from individual reading, a group Bible study offers an ideal setting in which to achieve these aims. Encourage participants to bring their Bibles and read from Scripture during the session. Invite participants to consider the following guidelines as they participate in the group:

Respect differences of interpretation and understanding.

Support one another with Christian kindness, compassion, and courtesy.

Listen to others with the goal of understanding rather than agreeing or disagreeing.

Celebrate the opportunity to grow in faith through Bible study.

Approach the Bible as a dialogue partner, open to the possibility of being challenged or changed by God's Word.

Recognize that each person brings unique and valuable life experiences to the group and is an important part of the community.

Reflect theologically—that is, be attentive to three basic questions: What does this say about God? What does this say about me/us? What does this say about the relationship between God and me/us?

Commit to a lived faith response in light of insights you gain from the Bible. In other words, what changes in attitudes (how you believe) or actions (how you behave) are called for by God's Word?

Group Sessions

The group sessions, like the chapters themselves, are built around three sections: "Claim Your Story," "Enter the Bible Story," and "Live the Story." Sessions are designed to move participants from an awareness of their own life story, issues, needs, and experiences into an encounter and dialogue with the story of Scripture and to make decisions integrating their personal stories and the Bible's story.

The session plans in the following pages will provide questions and activities to help your group focus on the particular content of each chapter. In addition to questions and activities, the plans will include chapter title, Scripture, and faith focus.

Here are things to keep in mind for all the sessions:

Prepare Ahead

Study the Scripture, comparing different translations and perhaps a paraphrase.

Read the chapter, and consider what it says about your life and the Scripture.

Gather materials such as large sheets of paper or a markerboard with markers.

Prepare the learning area. Write the faith focus for all to see.

Welcome Participants

Invite participants to greet one another.

Tell them to find one or two people and talk about the faith focus.

Ask: What words stand out for you? Why?

Guide the Session

Look together at "Claim Your Story." Ask participants to give their reactions to the stories and examples given in each chapter. Use questions from the session plan to elicit comments based on personal experiences and insights.

Ask participants to open their Bibles and "Enter the Bible Story." For each portion of Scripture, use questions from the session plan to help participants gain insight into the text and relate it to issues in their own lives.

Step through the activity or questions posed in "Live the Story." Encourage participants to embrace what they have learned and to apply it in their daily lives.

Invite participants to offer their responses or insights about the boxed material in "Across the Testaments," "About the Scripture," and "About the Christian Faith."

Close the Session
Encourage participants to read the following week's Scripture and chapter before the next session.
Offer a closing prayer.

1. Samuel's Journey With God
1 Samuel 1–15

Faith Focus
When life takes unexpected turns, we must remain engaged with God to move—however haltingly—toward God's purposes.

Before the Session
Read the first fifteen chapters of First Samuel in preparation for this session. Reflect on how you would characterize your own experience of faith. Locate copies of a hymnal with the hymn "Come, Thou Font of Every Blessing." Obtain paper and pencils or pens for participants. Read the two passages you will read aloud with the group for the imaginative visualization (1 Samuel 1:1-8 and 1 Samuel 1:9-28). The first passage in particular has some names that may be challenging to pronounce.

Claim Your Story
Give each person a sheet of paper and a pencil or pen and invite them to jot down times in their lives when God seemed near and other times when God seemed distant or unavailable to them. How do they describe the experiences of faith over their lifetime? As a journey, or in some other way? Ask: Would you describe yourself as spiritual? As religious? As both? The study writer reminds us that the characters in biblical stories struggled just as we do in discerning God's purposes for their lives. The stories in the Bible that tell of their struggles are places where we can connect with the ups and downs of our own spiritual journeys.

Enter the Bible Story
Invite participants to open their Bibles to the Book of Judges. Ask a volunteer to read aloud Judges 2:16-23. Persons who were judges functioned for Israel as leaders during this period. Then ask volunteers to read aloud Judges 2:11; 3:12; 4:1; 6:1; 10:6; and 13:1. Point out that the books of Samuel and Kings, those addressed in this study, are part of what is called the Deuteronomistic History, along with the books of Joshua and Judges. These verses from Judges underscore the pattern of rejection, suffering, and repentance that also emerges in Samuel and Kings.

Read aloud 1 Samuel 1:1-8, and then ask for reflections from the group. Point out the study writer's observation that this story follows a familiar scriptural pattern. What do participants recall about the stories of Sarah, Rachel, and Elizabeth?

Divide the group into smaller groups of three. In each group, ask one person to listen from the perspective of Hannah, one from Eli's viewpoint, and one from Elkanah's. Read aloud the remainder of Chapter 1. Have the small groups discuss the passage from their assigned viewpoint, encouraging them to take into account the study writer's observations about this passage.

To put the call of Samuel into context, ask the group to silently read Chapter 2 from verse 12 to the end of the chapter. How would participants characterize the boy Samuel as he grew? What about the sons of Eli? Call the group's attention to the second-to-last paragraph under the heading "Samuel's Rise to Prominence" (page 14) where the study writer mentions the ultimate fate of Eli's sons. Invite the group to quickly scan Chapters 4–7 and to briefly summarize the account of what happened to the ark of the covenant. The study writer observes that this narrative connects with stories from Judges when the people repeatedly failed to live up to the covenant. In what ways?

Summarize for the group the information about the people's demand for a king (page 15). Divide the group into two smaller groups. Invite participants to imagine Saul is up for reelection as king. Ask everyone to read over the information in 1 Samuel 9–15. Assign to one group the task of being Saul's campaign managers, and ask that they write an ad presenting Saul in the best light possible. Ask the other group to pretend to be the opposing party's campaign managers. Have the groups share their completed ads with the whole group. On balance, what is their assessment of Saul?

Live the Story

Read aloud the call of Samuel, 3:1-18. Ask participants to refer to responses they made at the beginning of the session of times when they sensed God's presence or absence. Was that sense clear at the time, or is it only in looking back that they can discern this? Have there been times when God's voice seemed clear to them, or has God's call more often been less than clear? Does discerning God's purpose for us always happen quickly or has it been more an experience of gradual and continual discernment?

Ask a volunteer to summarize what happens in 7:3-11. Then read aloud verses 12-14 and the study writer's observations about the Ebenezer in "About the Christian Faith" (page 14). Sing together "Come, Thou Font of Every Blessing" and close by reading Hannah's prayer (2:1-10) aloud, reflecting on the study writer's question: "How do Hannah's prayers help you share your own struggles with God?"

2. Living Faithfully
1 Samuel 16–31

Faith Focus

Our faithfulness to God and to others is sometimes the only thing we can control; but in the end, it is enough.

Before the Session

Read over 1 Samuel 16–31 in preparation for this session. Have available the ads the group composed in Session 1. On a large sheet of paper, print the following: "God grant me the serenity to accept the things I cannot change, courage to change the things I can, and wisdom to know the difference." On another large sheet of paper, print these two headings: "David the Musician/ Armor Bearer" and "David the Giant Killer." Post the sheet prominently in the room, and provide some felt-tipped markers. Obtain paper and pens or pencils.

Claim Your Story

Tell participants that the posted prayer is called the Serenity Prayer and is the first portion of a prayer attributed to the theologian Reinhold Niebuhr. It is used by twelve-step groups such as Alcoholics Anonymous. Invite participants to reflect on a time or times when they wished they could control how others behaved and a time when they had to face responsibility for their own behavior in a relationship. How do we determine what we can control and what we cannot? Would they agree that when we are in a faithful relationship with God, it's easier to be faithful (and responsible) in our relationships with others?

Enter the Bible Story

Ask volunteers from the two groups from last session who wrote positive and negative ads for Saul to read those aloud. Then ask a volunteer to read aloud 1 Samuel 15:35. Have the group take turns reading aloud the story of David's anointing, 16:1-13. Together, compose a positive campaign ad for David emphasizing his worthiness to be king and a negative ad pointing out his deficiencies. In what ways was David an unexpected choice? If the choice of a new king were handled like a presidential campaign, would one of David's brothers have been a more suitable candidate? Why?

Divide the group into two smaller groups and assign one of the following passages to each: 16:14-23 and 17:1–18:5. In these quite different accounts, the strongest correlation is that each presents David in a positive light and Saul in a negative one. Ask each group to read its assigned scriptural account and the information at "David Arrives at the Royal Court" (page 19) about it, and then to enter details about David revealed in their passage on the large sheet of paper.

Compare the two pictures of David. What are the inconsistencies between the accounts? What character traits seem to be comparable?

Invite the group to read the information under the headings "For Saul, Friendship Turns to Enmity" (page 21) and "For David, Loyalty Was Foremost" (page 22), as well as the related Scripture passages. Give participants paper and pencil or pen, and ask them to jot down episodes in David's life from the corresponding passages, using just a phrase to identify each episode. After allowing time to work, say that David's life would make an exciting miniseries. Head a sheet of paper "From Shepherd to King," and announce that the group is going to create an outline for this proposed miniseries. Print under the title the following: "David is anointed," "David kills Goliath," and "David the armor bearer plays music for Saul." Invite the group to continue the outline by naming (in just a phrase) the next episodes in David's life. List them down the sheet. Discuss what these incidents in David's life reveal about David. Explain that David was more concerned about his own actions in the moment than about Saul's in the past, and that while he could not control what Saul did, he could be responsible for his own actions. Does the group agree that these events are evidence of that perspective? How did David's actions of loyalty reveal concern for others?

Look at the sidebar, "Jesus Uses David as an Illustration" (page 24). Ask volunteers to read aloud 2 Samuel 21:1-6 and Mark 2:23-28. Does religious practice exist to serve the legitimate needs of people? Is there ever a time when religious practice should take precedence?

Live the Story

Distribute paper and pencils or pens. Invite participants to jot down the categories of family and friends, community, church, the nation, the world, the whole creation. Ask them to reflect on what things in these categories are out of their control to change. Then invite them to consider where, in each of these categories, they can do something to effect change. Where do they find the strength to do these things? What would constitute faithful living?

Close by praying together the portion of the Serenity Prayer you posted.

3. The Challenge of Blessings
2 Samuel 1–10

Faith Focus
God blesses us so that we can extend blessing to others, even those who may have wronged us in the past.

Before the Session
On a large sheet of paper, print the open-ended prompt, "If I Won the Lottery, I'd . . ." If you like, make arrangements to play the song "If I Had a Million Dollars," by the group Bare Naked Ladies, available from ITunes or as a video from YouTube. Have some self-stick notes and pens available. Also, post again the storyboard outline of David's life. If needed, add another large blank sheet of paper.

Claim Your Story
On self-stick notes, invite participants to respond to the open-ended prompt and stick their responses to the sheet of paper. If desired, play the recording of "If I Had a Million Dollars." Read some of the responses aloud. Ask: How would you characterize our responses? Are some of them designed to "share the wealth" or are they generally self-serving? Are any of our responses designed to give us power over other people? Did anyone suggest he or she might give some of the money to someone who has wronged them in the past?

Although David's ascendency to the throne may not exactly parallel winning the lottery, his journey from tending sheep to being the king was about as likely as a lottery win. How David responded to this blessing and to those who had wronged him is central to this session.

Enter the Bible Story
Invite a volunteer to read aloud the death of Saul as recorded in 1 Samuel 31:1-6. Then have someone read 2 Samuel 1:6-10. How do the two accounts differ? How would participants account for these differences? Can they be attributed to the "fog of war" or were other motivations at play, as the study writer suggests? If so, what are those motivations? How did David respond to Saul's death?

Where have we seen the cycles of violence played out in our communities? Nationally? Globally? Would participants agree that the only way to break the cycle of vengeance is to multiply the good things we receive by using them to benefit others?

Divide the group into two smaller groups. Assign one group 2 Samuel 2–4 and the text under the heading "Israel Descends Into Civil War" (page 27). To the other, assign the text under the heading "David Consolidates His Rule" (page 29) and 2 Samuel 5–8. Invite each group to generate a list of events in David's life and add them to the outline for the storyboard. Also, ask them to share any points the study writer makes. What distinguished the way David approached war and how he consolidated his power?

Explore together two accounts from those lists that illustrate unexpected twists. On a large sheet of paper, print the Hebrew word *beth*. Invite participants to name the various meanings for this word included on page 30. What did David plan to build as a way of sharing his blessings? Invite the group to talk about times when their congregation responded to God's blessings by expanding the church building. What happened? Have there been times when the congregation responded to God's blessings by expanding those blessings to include the larger community? How did God turn the tables on David's expectation that he would build a house for God?

Look together at the story of how David dealt with Mephibosheth (Chapter 9). What did Mephibosheth fear would happen when he was summoned by David? How did David share blessings with Mephibosheth, and how did that overturn Mephibosheth's expectations? Invite the group to reflect on those persons or groups they might consider to be enemies. Ask someone to summarize the information in the sidebar "Faithful Love" (page 31) about the meaning of the word *chesed*. In considering our enemies, how do we reconcile the tension between the two strands of meaning? How do we hold others accountable in love and at the same time demonstrate unconditional care for them as human beings? Or is this even possible?

Live the Story

Most of us are amazingly blessed just by virtue of having been born in this time and place, especially in comparison with most of the world's people. Ask participants to name aloud blessings they have received, material and otherwise. Then invite them to extend their hands in silence and imagine those blessings resting in the palms of their hands. Ask them to close their hands tightly and bring them up to their chests, and to imagine they are going to hold on tightly to all that they have, sharing only with members of their immediate family. Then invite them to extend their hands and open them wide, imagining that they are sharing blessings freely with those in the community and beyond.

Close by giving thanks to God for blessings received and blessings shared.

4. Accountable Forgiveness
2 Samuel 11–24

Faith Focus

A grateful response to God's gracious forgiveness involves acceptance of both God's judgment and the consequences of our wrongdoings, as well as a commitment to mend our ways.

Before the Session

Be aware that there may be participants who have experienced trauma such as domestic violence or child abuse. The mantra of "forgive and forget" may be far more complex and problematic for these persons than for others.

Post the outline of the storyboard of David's life. On a large sheet of paper, print the following: "To say 'just forgive and forget' can be an expression of cheap grace." Obtain paper and pens or pencils for participants. Prepare a sign on a large sheet of paper with the following disclaimer: "The following narrative contains content suitable for mature audiences. Viewer discretion is advised." Have available one copy of the participants' pages from Session 3. Get a playground ball to use in telling the story of Amnon.

Claim Your Story

With a show of hands, ask participants to make a forced choice on the statement you posted about forgiving and forgetting. If someone does not raise a hand in either agreement or disagreement, ask that person to choose the response that resonates the most. Invite volunteers to explain why they agreed or disagreed. As you read aloud the questions posed by the study writer under "Claim Your Story" (page 33), ask participants to jot down their responses on paper. Ask one or two persons to share a time when being forgiven led to inner peace.

Enter the Bible Story

Call attention to the outline on the storyboard of David's life that the group has been creating. David's life is a story worthy of being a miniseries. Often when a new episode is about to be shown, it is introduced with the words "Previously on _____," which is then followed by brief clips of the story so far. Ask participants to take turns reading the phrases outlining episodes in David's life as if they were narrating such an introduction. Then have someone read the first paragraph under "Enter the Bible Story" (page 34) aloud. Often a few episodes into a miniseries the dramatic action kicks up a notch. The same is true of David's story. Display the disclaimer statement.

Divide the group into four small groups or pairs. Each group or pair will consider one of the four episodes in the story of David and Bathsheba: David

Commits Adultery With Bathsheba (11:1-13); David Has Uriah Killed (11:14-27); Nathan Condemns David (12:1-15a); Bathsheba's Child Dies (12:15b-25). Each small group is to read the Scripture and any relevant information in the study guide and then formulate some discussion questions about this portion of the story. Discuss each subgroup's questions in the total group. What kind of love is evidenced in this narrative? Does David demonstrate *chesed* as he has in previous episodes? Is this simply about lust or power? Is it true that while forgiveness makes possible renewed relationship, it cannot wipe out the consequences of the acts?

Have participants move into a circle. Listen as a volunteer reads the sidebar about *chesed* from Session 3 (page 31). On paper, chart the progression of human evil the study writer includes in the first paragraph under the heading "The Price for David's Sin" ("Sexual infidelity leads to incestuous rape . . ." [page 37]). Participants will now sketch out the story of Amnon, Tamar, David, and Absalom as recorded in 2 Samuel 14–20. Encourage them to take a few moments to read over the portion of the study that details the story (pages 38-40). Begin by saying "Amnon fell in love with his half sister, Tamar." Toss the playground ball to someone, who will then add the next detail and toss the ball to another participant. Continue until everyone has added something and the entire story has been told (in a small group, participants will each tell several details).

How does the group respond to the observation that David extended only unconditional love to Amnon and Absalom, while they needed a love strong enough to hold them accountable for their actions? How might the story have been different if both aspects of *chesed* had played a part?

Live the Story

Ask participants to revisit the questions they considered at the beginning of the session, as well as the questions posed under "Live the Story" (page 40-41). The study writer suggests that there must be a balance between giving/receiving forgiveness and requiring/accepting responsibility. Ask the group to name where in our own lives—in our family and workplace—the lessons of this biblical story apply. What does this story call for in the life of the church? Does the community suffer if the full aspects of *chesed* are not applied to difficult situations?

5. Solomon—The Good, the Bad, and the Ugly
1 Kings 1–11

Faith Focus
Faithfulness to God enables us to identify attractive but false contenders and assert anew our complete loyalty to the one true God.

Before the Session
Do some research about what work your denomination is doing on fairly traded goods and other issues related to fair labor practices and wages and situations of forced labor. Obtain a large sheet of paper and a felt-tipped marker. Also, have drawing paper and crayons or markers for participants.

Claim Your Story
Invite participants to name the latest winners of the TV shows *American Idol* or *Dancing with the Stars* and list these on a large sheet of paper. Also list prominent sports and film or music stars. Ask participants also to candidly name, popcorn style, things in their lives they value the most.

Which of these people and things do we set up as idols in our culture? What kinds of values do they represent? In what ways, and why, can some of these things threaten to derail our spiritual lives?

Enter the Bible Story
What does the group first think of when they hear the name "King Solomon"? Most likely, some will remember the story of the two mothers who claimed the same child as their own, or perhaps the words of Jesus comparing the lilies of the fields with Solomon's splendor. The study writer speculates that perhaps the first false god to lure Solomon was that of royal power. What events in Solomon's ascension to the throne lead to that conclusion?

Divide the group into smaller groups of three and assign one of the following passages to each person in the groups: 1 Kings 3:16-28; 4:1-20; 4:29-34. Ask participants to read their assigned verses and then to summarize for the other two in their small group how Solomon showed wisdom. Together, discuss the conditional nature of Solomon's wisdom. To what degree is our ability to think or act wisely in making decisions and taking actions conditional on a faithful relationship with God?

Have the group silently read the information under the heading, "Solomon Builds the Temple" (page 46). Ask participants to quickly scan 1 Kings 5–9 and then name examples of the costly materials used to build the Temple and the palace. Have them identify what other wealth Solomon accrued. Then ask volunteers to read aloud the following: 2 Samuel 20:24; 1 Kings 9:15-22; 12:1-4, 15-17; 6:38–7:1; and 8:1-12, as well as the sidebar about corvée labor (page 47).

Though Solomon acted with the best of intentions, still he used the abominable tactic of forced labor to achieve his ends. Discuss together whether there are certain goods or services that we enjoy, perhaps unknowingly, at the expense of others. How do we find out if goods or products we purchase have been produced by forced labor or in exploitative labor situations? What can we do to remedy these injustices? Share the information you discovered about work your denomination may be doing on exploitative and forced labor and fair trade. How do our personal lifestyle choices around consumption have an impact on these issues?

What might have been the costs to the people of Israel of the ways Solomon achieved great wealth and the extravagance he exhibited? What might have been the cost to Solomon's relationship with God? Where do we see evidence of extravagant expenditure today by the powerful at the expense of others? Where do we see it in the church? What factors should congregations take into account when considering whether to build expensive new church buildings?

Although Solomon failed to be faithful in his relationship with God and allowed himself to be seduced by other gods, there is no evidence that he ever completely rejected that relationship. Like Solomon, do we fail to make the connections ourselves between our allegiance to other "gods" and a failure in our relationship to the Holy One? What price do we pay?

Live the Story

The study writer observes that the power and allure of an idol is never in the image itself, but in the value or thing it represents. Distribute drawing paper and crayons or markers. Call attention to the list of "idols" participants generated at the beginning of the session. Invite them to choose one "idol" that is personally tempting or seductive and print it in the center of the paper. Around that word, ask them to print the values this idol embodies. Encourage them to consider prayerfully what place this idol occupies in their lives and how it impacts their relationship with God. Pray together that our relationship with God will be strengthened and that other competing commitments will not assume the central place that God should hold in our lives.

6. Listening to the Prophets
1 Kings 12–22

Faith Focus
God provides messengers who equip us to recognize our harmful behaviors so that we can recommit to living faithfully and purposefully according to God's plan.

Before the Session
On posterboard or a piece of cardboard, prepare a sign that reads, "The End of the World Is at Hand," and attach a dowel or a yardstick to the back. Also have available for participants sheets of posterboard or cardboard, felt-tipped markers, and yarn or dowels and tape.

Claim Your Story
Point out the sign you prepared. Ask the group if they have heard predictions of the end of the world. Some may be familiar with the phenomenon from 2012 mentioned on page 53. Others may remember the billboards worldwide that predicted that the world would end May 21, 2011. Invite participants to describe what they think the role was of prophets in the Old Testament. Were they predicting the end of the world or the coming of the Messiah? Or was their role something else? Ask participants to respond to the question: "How have biblical prophecies affected your outlook?" Do the contemporary end-of-the-world predictions reflect biblical understandings?

Enter the Bible Story
Briefly review for the group what the study writer has to say about the conception of prophets in Israel and how it differs from the contemporary understandings on which end-time predictions are based. In this session we will examine several prophets, both named and unnamed, in this portion of First Kings.

Invite a volunteer to review the courses of action enumerated in the last session that led to the division of the kingdom following Solomon's death. Ask the group to form pairs to look at the stories of two prophets in the midst of this division of the kingdoms. One person in each pair will look at the story of Shemaiah (12:20b-24) and the other the story of the unnamed man of God (13:1-10). Invite each pair to consider the stories and to answer these questions: What was the response to the prophet's message, and what was the result?

Form three small groups to look at the two stories of Elijah. Ask someone to read aloud 1 Kings 18:1-19. Then ask one group to explore part 1 of the story of Elijah and the priests of Baal (18:20-46), another to look at part 2 (19:1-18), and a third to examine the story of Naboth's vineyard (21:1-29). Encourage the groups to create some way to present their part of the narrative to the total group. It could be as simple as reading the account aloud or it could be acting it out or some other way. Following the presentations, discuss the intent in each case of the prophet's actions and words. What happened? Were the people or their rulers turned completely back to God?

Consider together the account of Jehoshaphat, Ahab, and Micaiah (22:1-38). Ask one or more volunteers to read the passage aloud. Invite the group to consider what to make of this strange story. How does one tell if a person is being influenced by a lying spirit? Can the group cite examples of people who sincerely believe themselves to be messengers of God? The study writer suggests that we should measure the messages of such people with what we know to be a faithful way to live. Can such a person demonstrate a life lived with integrity and faithfulness and still be mistaken in his or her message?

Live the Story

The study writer suggests that the primary concern of the ancient prophets of Israel and Judah was with the lives of their contemporaries, not with the future, that they were less concerned with foretelling than forth-telling the truth. True prophets confront us with truths we would rather not hear and challenge us to change our behavior.

Distribute posterboard or cardboard and markers. Invite participants to compose messages about the situation in the world today. Encourage them to craft messages that challenge people to take responsibility and change their behavior in order to impact the way the world is. When their messages are done, participants can either attach dowels to the signs or use yarn to connect two sheets of posterboard to make placards they can wear. Silently process around your space displaying the prophetic messages. Or display the signs and have group members move around the space reading them and reflecting on their messages.

Ask the group to close with a time of prayer in which you read aloud the questions the study writer poses in the final paragraph (page 60), allowing time after each question for silent prayer.

7. Everyone's an Example, Whether Good or Bad
2 Kings 1–25

Faith Focus

Biblical models of both success and failure enable us to discern God's presence with us as we move into an uncertain future.

Before the Session

In advance of the session, cut two large paper doll shapes from large sheets of paper or make large outlines of a figure on the sheets. These will be used by two small groups to show positive and negative characteristics of Hezekiah and Josiah. If your group has more than about ten members, you may want to make additional outlines or cut-outs so the smaller groups will be no larger than five members. Provide felt-tipped markers for participants. Locate a hymnal with the hymn "Great Is Thy Faithfulness" for the closing.

Claim Your Story

Call the attention of the group to the question the study writer poses at the beginning of the second paragraph under "Claim Your Story" (page 61). Ask participants to pair up and identify some area of their lives where they need to get information about what is best in order to make an important decision or to address a pressing issue in their life. Ask them to discuss that issue with their partner and determine what questions they use to decide what is best. What factors might influence what questions they ask, and how do they determine what is best?

Enter the Bible Story

Tell the group that in this chapter they will explore the kings the writer of First and Second Kings identified as best and worst. This writer's criterion for making such a determination was the degree to which a king followed David's example in faithfulness to God. Why was every king in the northern Hebrew kingdom from Jeroboam to Hoshea on the "worst" list? Note for the group, just for general information, what the study writer has to say in the sidebar "Interpreting History Theologically" (page 62) about the structure of First and Second Kings. If participants were going to rate U.S. presidents according to best and worst, what criteria would they use? Invite them to name some criteria, and list these on a sheet of paper. Assuming participants named different ways to make this judgment, would they also differ in how they assess presidents?

Together, consider the story of Elisha. Ask someone to read aloud 1 Kings 19:16-21, where Elisha is introduced. Ask volunteers to add to this picture of Elisha some of the information on pages 63 and 64. Have group members read silently the passages cited in the study that show Elisha's relationships with both the rich and the poor.

Ask the group to listen as a volunteer reads aloud 2 Kings 5:1-27. What acts of Elisha are consistent with his faithfulness to God? What does the group make of the fact that Elisha performed miracles? The study writer observes that the absence of the miraculous—for example, the failure of someone to heal—does not equate with the absence of God. Do participants agree? When we encounter difficult experiences like a chronic illness or the unexpected death of a loved one, what steps can we take to discern God's presence? If we feel separated from God, does that mean that God is not there? Why?

Divide the group into two or more smaller groups of no more than five participants. To one group, assign Hezekiah, and to the other, Josiah. Give each group a paper doll cut-out or outline. Ask groups to use the material in the sections "Hezekiah" and "Josiah" (pages 64-68) to assess the faithfulness of their character, printing a list of positive characteristics on one side of the figure or outline and the negatives on the other side. When groups have completed their task, have each one share their lists with the total group. How do they define faithfulness? Would they agree with the study writer that being faithful to God is less about blind confidence that God will protect them from all harm and more about living in relationship with God? How is the cyclical pattern of Deuteronomistic History revealed in the stories of these kings?

Ask participants to read over the information about Jehoiachin (page 68). What element of hope that the cycle might just be broken is revealed in this account?

Live the Story

The study writer observes that each of the figures considered in this chapter lived in a time of uncertainty and upheaval. Invite the group to consider what examples of faithfulness are revealed in the lives of these people and what weaknesses in them they would like to avoid. What global and national uncertainties are a reality in our lives today? What personal upheavals and difficulties are we dealing with? How do we cultivate in ourselves a sense of God's presence and faithfulness?

Close by singing together the hymn "Great Is Thy Faithfulness" as an affirmation of those assurances.

8. Re-forming Community in the Context of Exile
First and Second Chronicles

Faith Focus

As we look to the past, our aim cannot be to return to it; faithful response in times that we feel "exiled" requires that we discern God's presence in our historical and cultural context today.

Before the Session

On a large sheet of paper, print the words "exile" and "emergent."

On another large sheet, head three columns with "David's Story," "Solomon's Story," and "The Story From Rehoboam to Cyrus." Locate a hymnal with the hymn "The Church's One Foundation."

Claim Your Story

Call attention to the words *exile* and *emergent*. How would participants use these two terms to describe what is happening to the church? Would they agree that while the church has not been literally exiled from our society, it does not occupy the position or enjoy the status it once did? Describe emergent churches—typically (though not exclusively) new church developments with younger members that make heavy use of media and social networking. What direction is the church moving in? Can we say definitely what the church will be like in the future? Should there be some grounding in the past? Why?

Enter the Bible Story

Ask participants to scan the information in the first two paragraphs under "Enter the Bible Story" (pages 71-72). Ask a volunteer to summarize briefly the context in which Chronicles was written. What was the question behind the writing of Chronicles? Do we have a similar question in the church today?

In the first seven sessions of this study, we tried to enter the Bible story to use it as a lens to both discern God's presence and activity in our lives and to provide a structure for us to tell of our own spiritual journeys. In this session, the group will try to watch what the writer is doing rather than what he has done.

Note that Chronicles not only overlaps the period covered by the books of Samuel and Kings, it also borrows from those books, in some places word-for-word. We can learn from what the writer of Chronicles borrows, decides to leave out, and adds to the work of his predecessors. Invite the group to name the aspects of Chronicles noted in the study and list them on a large sheet of paper (interest in the Davidic dynasty and the history of Judah and concern primarily for the religious life of the people [pages 73-74]). What is left out of Chronicles? What is emphasized? Sometimes it is suggested that Chronicles attempts to whitewash the more sordid aspects of David's life. How does the group respond to what the study writer suggests in response to that critique? What is the value for us in attending to our relationship with God and how we worship God? How can we recognize God's presence in a changed religious landscape? How can we be spared from repeating mistakes we have made in the past?

Chronicles is divided into four major sections. What is the biblical writer trying to do with the first section, the genealogies (1 Chronicles 1–9)? Look at the three other sections listed on the sheet of paper: David's Story, Solomon's Story, and The Story From Rehoboam to Cyrus. Invite the group to name the ways each of these remaining three sections emphasizes the centrality of the Temple within the life of the people, and list these in the appropriate column.

Ask participants to read over the material about the three themes that emerge from the two books of Chronicles. Note that the themes offer us only a pattern since our circumstances are quite different from those of the time of Chronicles. Have participants jot down on paper one way each of these themes might inform the church of today—one lesson we might learn, a strategy we might employ, or an affirmation to which we might cling. After allowing time for reflection, review each theme and invite volunteers to share their thoughts about each.

Live the Story

"Continuity always requires connection with the past, but if it does not reflect change, then it is not really 'continuity' but rather simply 'identity'" (page 78). How does the group respond? If moving into the future requires leaving something behind, what determines what moves ahead and what is left behind?

Ask participants to read in the "Live the Story" section (pages 78-79) the suggestion of retelling the history of the church in the West from the time of the Reformation. While this assignment is too daunting for your class timeframe, suggest that participants think about the history of the church within their own lifetimes—the changes the church has undergone, events that have occurred, and the historical context of those events. What would be the lessons learned, the patterns that aid discernment, and the signs of hope and encouragement?

Close by singing "The Church's One Foundation," remembering the history of God's people and affirming that in the midst of yet more uncertainty, God's people have hope for the future.

IMMERSE YOURSELF IN ANOTHER VOLUME

IMMERSION
Bible Studies

Available at Cokesbury and other booksellers

AbingdonPress.com

BKM126600001 PACP01238834-01

CPSIA information can be obtained at www.ICGtesting.com
Printed in the USA
LVOW04s0830281114

415617LV00001B/1/P